The Power to Change

The Power to Change

women in the third world redefine their environment

WOMEN'S FEATURE SERVICE

Zed Books Ltd
London and New Jersey

The Power to Change
was originally published in 1992 in India and S. Asia by

KALI FOR WOMEN
A 36 Gulmohar Park
New Delhi 110 049
India

and in 1993 by Zed Books Ltd., 57 Caledonian Road,
London N1 9BU, UK and 171, First Avenue, Atlantic
Highlands, New Jersey, 07716, USA in the rest of the world.

ISBN 1 85649 225 7 Hb
ISBN 1 85649 226 5 Pb

*Calaloguing-in-publication data can be obtained from the
British Library*

Lasertypeset by Vision Wordtronic Pvt. Ltd.,
111/56 Nehru Place, New Delhi 110 019
and printed by Raj Press, R-3, Inderpuri,
New Delhi 110 012, India

Contents

ACKNOWLEDGEMENTS

This book is a result of the imagination and hard work of many people. Those that have had a direct input are mentioned in the credit section; other individuals and institutions have made it possible for the Women's Feature Service (WFS) to become and continue as a reality.

Inter Press Service, the Third World news agency, housed the WFS as a project from 1978 to 1990 and enabled it to move into its own. With UNESCO, IPS took on the challenge of providing a framework in which the concerns voiced over the UN Decade for Women and the New International Information and Communication Order could be realised.

The WFS was created to accurately reflect the experiences, dreams and aspirations of women, in a development context. Both the NIICO and the UN Decade for Women, among others, have recognised the link between the portrayal of women in mainstream media and their status in societies.

It took a while for mainstream media to comprehend that the WFS material was more than about 'women's issues'. It was a progressive women's perspective that the service was offering, and one of a kind. We salute the more imaginative editors of news media who realised this and hope that many more will join the ranks, as is the case. The selections in the book have almost all appeared in one medium or another, some several times over, in different languages in the North and South.

The United Nations agencies, UNFPA, UNIFEM, UNESCO and UNICEF have financially supported the WFS. The development cooperation agencies of the governments of the Netherlands, Norway, Switzerland and Sweden have also financially contributed to its growth and development. The Dutch NGO, NOVIB, the EMW (Evangelisches Missionswerk) of Germany, KFO (Katholische Frauenbewegung Osterreiche) of Austria, United Methodist Board of Global Ministries, and the Sam Rubin Foundation have made important contributions to our day to day operations.

Other individuals and institutions have offered moral and professional support which has been invaluable. It goes without saying that the WFS could not have either come into existence or continued to grow and develop without the imagination, resilience and commitment of many, many people.

This book is a testimony to that.

Anita Anand
Director, WFS

May 1992

CREDITS

The authors of the features, regional overviews and the introduction have their credit lines. Over the years many others have brought their professional skills to the WFS and we would like to recognise them.

In Africa, the regional work has been coordinated from Harare, Zimbabwe. Colleen Lowe Morna has travelled, written, trained and coordinated the network more recently. Patricia Made, as the regional editor of Inter Press Service, has helped with back-up assistance. Before Colleen Morna, the regional work was managed and developed by Ruth Ansah Ayisi and Grace Mutwanda. Rokhaya Sarr of Senegal made a major contribution in creating a service from Francophone Africa.

In the Philippines, Manila-based journalists, Lorna Tirol and Olivia Tripon, have coordinated the work from the country, seeking out other women journalists, commissioning the features, sub-editing them, and enabling a steady flow of material from the Philippines.

Since 1986, New Delhi, India, has served as the regional centre for Asia. Sheela Reddy and Sujata Madhok have coordinated the work, with assistance from Anitha Pandey. And for a while, Sujata Madhok has served as the final editor of the English language material, an undertaking over and above her contract. Gouri Salvi, working out of the Delhi base, has managed the features from Africa, Latin America, the Caribbean and the Middle East, and been an invaluable member of the team.

IPS provided technical assistance to the WFS while it was a project of the news agency, in Rome. Roshan Lyman of TIPS (Technological Information Pilot System) set up the ISIS system and Daniella Vatter daringly took on the task of creating the dynamic database. The work was fine-tuned and further developed by the WFS technical consultant, Mahesh Uppal. John Clements of IPS provided an invaluable service by stocking all the WFS features in London, without being asked, and transferring them to us at a later stage.

In January 1991, the WFS moved its central management from Rome to Delhi, and became an independent organisation. Sheela Reddy and Patricia Baeza took on the responsibility of editors-in-chief of the service. The expanded WFS in Delhi was provided back-up service by Alka Chaurasia, Pooja Kapur, Taposhi Roychowdhary, Ina Sathe and Nikunj.

In New York, Rebecca Foster serves as the North American liaison point, and an important team member of the WFS since 1988.

In Latin America, where the WFS first started, the spadework of creating a regional presence was done in San Jose, Costa Rica, by Isabel Ovares, succeeded by Thais Aguilar. Magaly Chaves, Vera Morales, Lisa Shallott, Christia Green, all played and play a major role in translating, editing and providing administrative assistance to the regional network. Italy-based Patricia Baeza accepted a major challenge in temporarily relocating to the region and helping build a stronger presence.

The WFS regions that do not feature in this collection are the Caribbean, the Middle East and North Africa. There is a service from these areas and Suzanne Francis of Jamaica and Ihsan Bouabaid of Morocco are to be recognised for this.

There are many others who have assisted us in small and not so small ways, far too many to name. But the bulk of the credit needs to go to the central and regional management of Inter Press Service, and the editors, translators and staff who have offered assistance, suggestions and advice at all times.

Ritu Menon, who suggested this book be put together, has in her personal, professional and political capacity been an inspiration for the WFS.

And finally, all the women journalists who have made a major effort in reaching into themselves and outside of themselves to do the kind of writing that makes the WFS the kind of network it is.

IN THE FIELD

You are always in the field
Carrying
Loads on the head
A baby asleep on the back
Pounding
Clearing
Tilling
My mother, you are always working
So much that I can't even tell the
difference
Between
You and the fields

What a strange beauty

A.R.H. Attah, Ghana

INTRODUCTION

The Women's Feature Service was launched in 1978 with the goal of creating a space in mainstream media, for women's voices to be heard. What started as a service in which the focus was 'women's issues', 13 years later has emerged as a service in which the focus is on development issues from a progressive women's, or gender, perspective.

A gender perspective is one in which women's knowledge, experiences and perceptions are given validity and allowed to come to the fore in analysing and presenting issues. It is a perspective that is often given second class status, and the struggle to make it a part of the mainstream has had to be deliberate. A progressive perspective insists that changes occurring in society, planned or unplanned, have to be viewed critically, with the objective of taking people forward, not backward, and that a consideration of human dignity is essential in all change.

The WFS' need to insist that the service is not about 'women's issues' but about development from a progressive women's perspective, emerged alongside the history of several movements which impacted one another. The women's movement, grassroots and people's movements, national liberation struggles, all stressed the need for people to be treated with dignity, irrespective of their gender, race, class or colour. And with these, and sometimes overlapping, was the development movement.

Of development — and women

Planned development since the early 1950s, in the North and South, was based on many theories, but predominantly, the 'trickle-down theory' which assumed that as the standard of living·of nations arose, the benefits would accrue to all, including women. This belief was based on the presumption that all are equal, in spite of the fact that history had proved otherwise and continues to do so. At the same time, women who were participating in many national struggles in the North and South were slowly beginning to realise that they were often being marginalised, even as their nations marched forward. National movements to end colonialism and racism, in which women played a prominent role, never fully accepted them as equal partners, especially when it came to power and authority. The women, for their part, were torn between their loyalty to anti-racist and anti-colonialist struggles, and their personal needs, which invariably got lower priority. Men exploited and reinforced women's guilt and fear by advocating that they not split the struggle by bringing in the 'woman question'.

Over a period of time women realised that they had to organise, separately, in order for their concerns to be addressed. Women's movements in the North and South, as well as women in the development movement, began examining the nature of their discrimination. In the late Sixties and early Seventies both movements began to come into their own, but it was not till the late Seventies that a feminist interjection was made into development, and development concerns incorporated into women's movements.

What seemed to have kept the two movements apart were the so-called 'women's issues' or the priorities of the women's movements: reproductive rights (abortion, contraception, childbirth), violence against women in and outside the home, sex discrimination, childcare, etc. Although society had as much responsibility for these issues, institutionalised patriarchy did not feel the need to, and would not, address them. Development policy and planning, from which women were systematically excluded, did not reflect these concerns either, or see them as development issues.

While women within the development movement and those in the women's movements were organsing in their own spheres, as well as together, moves were also being made at an international level. The United Nations, the only international body with a membership of national governments, had been an advocate and pressure group for women as far back as 1945, when the UN Charter stated the principle of equality as "without distinction as to race, sex, language or religion". The UN has also played a role in two vital areas: de jure equality, by setting up an international legal framework, and de facto equality, through raising of public awareness and a commitment to changing long-standing traditions and attitudes that perpetuate discrimination. Since the adoption of the Charter, the UN has established mechanisms to ensure that the women's agenda is incorporated in various spheres, in and outside the UN system.

In 1946 the Commission on the Status of Women (one of the first UN commissions) was created as a subsidiary body of the Economic and Social Council, to formulate guidelines and actions to improve women's status in the economic, political, social, cultural and educational fields. The Committee on the Elimination of Discrimination Against Women was established in 1982 as the treaty monitoring body for the Convention on the Elimination of All Forms of Discrimination against Women. It keeps track of compliance with the Convention's provisions by over 100 ratifying countries. The Convention is the single most authoritative legal document to emerge from the United Nations Decade for Women; it sets standards for countries to improve the living and working conditions of women, and its 30 articles cover civil, political and reproductive rights.

In the Fifties and Sixties the UN approach to women was more protective than status oriented; it was only in the Seventies, when women critiqued mainstream development from a gender perspective that the UN felt a more direct approach was needed, and declared 1975 as the International Year for Women with a conference at Mexico City, Mexico. Following the conference, a Decade for Women (1976-1985) was announced, whose objective was to survey the status of women

in all member nations of the UN and to make recommendations to the UN, international bodies and member governments, to improve the status of women.

During the deliberations of the Decade, in which two other
international conferences were held (Copenhagen, 1980 and
Nairobi 1985), something very significant occurred, which
brought together the concerns of the women's movement as
well as the UN's agenda for the conference. Would the issue
of violence against women, for example — be it rape, incest,
sexual harassment and other forms of mental and physical
abuse — be part of the peace section of the conference agenda?
What about reproductive rights? The situation of women in the
informal economy, the role of multinationals? As in other UN
conferences, regional and political conflicts such as the Arab-
Israeli question and apartheid were an undercurrent in the
day-to-day proceedings of the meetings. But what did they
have to do with women? Plenty, as it turned out. Women, or
their male delegates from these areas, pointed out that there
was no way that the status of women in these regions would
improve unless fundamental change was brought about, i.e, a
homeland for the Palestinians and majority rule for South
Africa. While this made evident sense it had to be stressed that
although homeland and majority rule were essential, they did
not by themselves guarantee equity for women, for which
reason a gender perspective had to be built into any analysis
of the issue and finally into the conference document.

The use of terms such as sexism, feminism and patriarchy as
institutionalised obstacles to the change in the status of women
raised hackles among some country delegations, evoking
some of the best feminist writing on the subject. Where
colonialism, racism and imperialism were accepted by delegates, it was obvious that there was a high level of discomfort
with some of the analyses put forward by feminists for the
official agenda of the conference.

The point being made, for historical reasons, is that the
Forward Looking Strategies, or the document that emerged as
a consensus of the conference was a landmark, in that it
incorporated — unlike any other UN document from a UN

conference — the concerns of all women, in a *socio-political and economic context*. It also reflected the tremendous level of organising that had gone on during the Decade in different countries, to ensure that the various and different levels of women's interests were represented. The Decade also laid the groundwork for analyses, policy recommendations, implementation and action on women and development, that made it possible for women and communities to play the role they have in bringing their issues to the forefront of the development debate.

What the Decade and the *Forward Looking Strategies* revealed was that development concerns cannot and should not be compartmentalised. The document highlighted the fact that unless the everyday preoccupations of women (not 'women's issues') were addressed, no real development was possible; and that these preoccupations are not different from men's: the need for shelter, water, food, health care, childcare, literacy, income, human dignity, and a life free from physical and mental violence. The women's movements were saying to developmentalists that a serious erosion of women's rights was taking place, in spite of planned development, and very often, precisely because of it.

At the same time, however, women also realised that organising around the issues of reproductive rights, violence against women, childcare and so on had limited scope, unless the issues of international and national priorities on military spending and nuclearisation, regional conflicts, debt, trade, etc., were also addressed. It would be of little consequence for women to be organising and protesting, generating their gender perspective on development, while planners went about their business, as usual.

The lack of a gender perspective in development was also partly a result of there being few or no women in the public domain, and a failure to recognise that women had a valuable contribution to make, from where they were. Their economic contribution through their labour, in and outside the home, was vital for development. The so-called 'invisibility' of women was the result of a gendered division of labour which glorified women's roles as home-makers and child-rearers, while simultaneously devaluing their productive labour. This invisibility was carried even further by census and policy documents which not only ignored women but, in a curious turnabout, even disqualified them for participation in public and political life.

This very marginalisation, however, enabled women to come together, to think and act collectively, to resist, to create a movement against the system. This resistance moreover enabled an unconventional analysis of problems and of legal, educational, religious, and government institutions, all of which are patriarchal, exclusive and privileged by power.

The inadequate representation and recognition of women's contribution in development policy and practice has much to do with the poor results it has shown. Low growth rates and increasing disparities between the rich and the poor have led developmentalists to re-examine predominant or widely accepted theories and practices. Women and alternative organisations have also realised that organising outside the system can only go so far. Unless accountability is sought by citizens to achieve their fundamental rights, little will change. The individuals and groups serving as intermediaries between the system and the disenfranchised have become a vocal and potent force; activists, organisers, non-governmental organisations, they work for equitable social change.

Documenting change

Development journalism is more than just reporting on development issues. For what exactly is a development issue? The WFS has chosen to define development as a social, political and economic process of change which, to be just and sustainable, must ensure the participation of all class, race and gender groups.

We feel that our objective can best be met by focusing on events not just as events, but as harbingers of change that has happened or is about to happen. It is not the event itself that makes the story, but what shapes the event and the processes it sets in motion. In this approach are woven values, aspirations, power, priorities, and what happens when an element of change is introduced — when, in fact, development takes place.

Furthermore, we choose to focus on those issues or aspects of issues that are not being addressed by mainstream media. The service would like to insist that women journalists enter arenas which have so far been a male reserve — trade, politics, economics — and in which a progressive women's perspective is desperately needed.

Women, who have so far been on the margin, need to be put at the centre of development theory and practice. The first step in enabling this is to recognise that men and women are affected differently by change, irrespective of heredity or environment. For example, the introduction of a new technology will be accepted differently by women and men. Let us take the case of reproductive technologies. Amniocentesis, a procedure to detect birth defects, also has the possibility of revealing the sex of a foetus. In many countries of the South where male children are preferred over female, the test is being used for sex selection and the aborting of female foetuses.

While it is difficult to take a position one way or another on this issue, one thing is clear: if women had been more involved in the research and development of the procedure, and the phenomenon of male child preference had been more widely known, perhaps the sex selection aspect of the test would not have been propagated. The problem lies in assuming that science and technolgy are gender neutral and that the implications of gender blindness are not thought through; for once the technology has been introduced, it is difficult to turn back the clock.

For the WFS to be a development service with a progressive women's perspective, has meant that writing on the environment was a natural, it was not an 'issue'. When women journalists were asked to write on development, as defined by the WFS, the challenges that women faced in their day to day lives often came under the category of 'environment'. In 1972 at the environment conference in Stockholm, the concerns articulated were certainly environmental — pollution, deforestation, the population explosion, wilderness, extinction of flora and fauna. When the North spoke of environment, the South viewed it as a capitalist plot, insisting that talk of reducing population growth or preserving forests were luxuries for the rich. At the same time the South, in its bid to catch up with post-colonial development had by and large (with the exception of a few countries) accepted the predominant notion of trickle-down development and embraced industrial growth. Shrinking resources versus increasing population was a delicate debate even then, and in the Nineties, it is just that much more volatile.

The politics of language plays a dual role: it is helpful, in that it clarifies, and unhelpful in that it tends to diffuse. In the numbers game, terms such as family planning (spacing children) versus population control (deliberately reducing or keeping down numbers of certain classes, colours, religions or sex) tend to polarise the situation. The concept of family planning was based on the fact that women needed a break from repeated childbirths that debilitated them physically and mentally. In the North, as increasing prosperity and development brought about adequate and reliable health care, women did not need more children, just that a few should survive. Old-age pension schemes, gainful employment, a high standard of living, access to education and information, and increased social security made for small families and a sharp drop in birth rates.

Birth control now came to be seen as desirable for the South where the newly independent ex-colonies were considered to be illiterate, disease-ridden, and with families that were far too large. The introduction of the family planning programmes for the South, as early as the Fifties, was thought of as a revolution that would cater to the changing needs of a neo-colonist population — changing from rural to urban, illiterate to educated and from producer to consumer, all perceived prerequisites for a small family.

Trends in migration — rural-urban, country-country and region to region — brought about by geo-political realities created a class of people that were viewed as 'the other'. It was these migrants who needed lower birth rates, should their potentially increasing numbers be used for political and economic leverage. For many women all over the North and South, the possibility of regulating fertility is a liberating notion; but enforced contraception, like enforced motherhood, once again robs them of control over their fertility, and family planning or population control, together with the new reproductive technologies became the new instruments of oppression. While family planning is a desirable goal, a kind of savagery has emerged in the zeal to control births, in which women's bodies are often viewed as mere machines to be poked, pried, manipulated and experimented on. Feminists are not against birth control, but call for more women- centred approaches in which they have more input at each stage, for the need to control births is very real.

Choices regarding reproduction are complex, in which values, lifestyles, personal preferences and priorities are intertwined. But whatever the perception of choices, women cannot participate as partners in development if their productive years are spent primarily in taking care of children and homes. The politics of housework and child-rearing have largely been unaddressed by environmentalists and developmentalists. Notions of equity are heard at forums and written into charters and recommendations, but very few organisations make it possible for women to participate in any real way or offer them economic compensation for childcare. For women to step into public life, men will have to take a step back, and accept more responsibility in the home than they currently do.

Witnessing change

If development is about change, and change almost always brings conflict, then constant communication is essential to check, affirm and ensure that there is a moving forward together. Towards this end, communication also becomes a process of reporting on change, making change, witnessing change and heralding change. It was these criteria that the WFS adopted for the material it provided to mainstream media, hoping it would create an awareness and discussion in the wider community. And as the features came in from the field, it became clear that something unique was going on. Women in almost all parts of the world, especially the South, where most of the features originated, were slowly taking control of their environment. Despite the fact that they had little or no access to and control over land, capital, technology, literacy, and the political process, they were working with what they had to redefine their environment.

What emerges from the WFS features is, predictably, a picture of suffering, deprivation and discrimination but, at the same time, tremendous resilience on the part of women to overcome this reality. The emergence and growth of national, regional and international non-governmental organisations has enabled women to have access to facilities for organising their lives and work. International donor agencies in their attempts to understand and support women, have played a major role in reversing the trend of inequitable development on the basis of gender. This has not been easy, for often, their own governments and the recipient governments they were in aid partnership with, were reluctant to deal with women as a separate category. Despite these objections, special funds for women and development were set aside, both for women-only projects and women in integrated development schemes. One way NGOs and donor agencies have worked, together and separately, is through projects, especially income-generating ones. The WFS, in its coverage of these projects, has viewed them as a means rather than an end to women being recognised as equal partners in development.

It is these projects that have brought women together, be it for sewing, knitting, weaving, mud stoves or tree planting, with a strong aspect of income generation. It is increasingly accepted that unless women have economic independence any talk of real change is futile. The effort to initiate projects for women has raised issues that have had to be tackled, one by one; the question of credit for instance, was constantly raised by women as a major obstacle to progress. Any enterprise requires capital and inputs; banks were reluctant to lend money to women who could not provide collateral, as often property was in the names of male family members. Initiatives such as special bank schemes for women in which NGOs acted as guarantors for the women, turned the situation around. Beginning with the Women's World Banking to local bank lending schemes such as the grameen banks, (or village) women have developed a solid reputation for repaying loans in record time.

And these are women micro-entrepreneurs, in small business, in the informal sector, mostly self-employed, who for years have lost out to middlemen, petty moneylenders and greed. Along with the ability to borrow money, women have collectivised to pool in their skills and experiences, products and resources, learning from each other and asking for skills they do not have. For example, when women in the informal sector came together to acquire loans, they realised that they needed marketing and money management skills, which often required literacy. Suddenly literacy, which may have been considered irrelevant, becomes priceless, a key to future independence. Again, once goods were produced, a market or an outlet was needed, which would link them to a wider circle of entrepreneurship for which they had to be equipped. Working class women have always had to take their children to work be it construction, vending or domestic labour or leave them with extended families, those that have them. But migrant women and families do not have access to such infrastructures and more and more organisations have begun to offer childcare facilities, knowing that unless this is done, women's productivity, and eventually their capacity to succeed, will suffer.

Most working class women have high birth rates and little access to decent family planning and counselling, and little mutuality in their personal lives. In the South high birth rates have meant many children are unwanted and, eventually, dumped. The alarming rise in street children, by choice or by force, the still more staggering number of children orphaned by war, drought, famine, floods and AIDS, is enough to shame the shameable. The high rate of abandoned and unprotected children makes them so dispensible that they easily become targets of rape, violence, abuse, and even death.

Women define their environment

When the United Nations Conference on Environment and Development scheduled for June 1992 in Rio de Janeiro, Brazil, was announced, the WFS felt that what was missing was a consistent gender perspective on the issues of environment and development; and, beyond the gender perspective, what was needed was a breaking open of the narrowly com-partmentalised 'issues' of environment. The WFS environment dossier, when put together, revealed features with a high level of organising around issues which, traditionally, would not be considered under environment. What came across loud and clear was the fact that women in the informal sector, as heads of households, as industrial workers when interviewed for the features, revealed how their lives had changed, what they thought were the reasons for it, and what they felt it would take to change the situation. Contrary to popular opinion, there was a lived understanding of the links between macro and micro, the larger systemic issues of poverty and the displacement caused by maldevelopment, and the tremendous indignity with which people had been treated.

The first culling of the material for the book was from the WFS production of 1990-91, and features with an overt 'environment' connection were selected. Then, for the same period, we took features that portrayed women and organisations getting together and defining their environment; and finally, we took material that satisfied both criteria, from 1988 onwards. Preference was given to features that had something new to say, where women and communities were taking control of the situation and challenging the status quo, where ordinary people were doing extraordinary things to refashion their lives. The material has been organised by region; Africa, Asia and Latin America, by virtue of the fact that they are at different stages of development, reflect these differences through the issues, preoccupations and styles of organising taken up.

This account is not intended to be comprehensive, either in scope or in coverage. It does not represent all countries or regions of the South, and often, it does not specifically feature every country even when very active struggles are taking place within it. Rather, the features selected tell stories of how situations create a context in which people respond. As such, instead of arbitrarily dividing the features into concepts, themes or problem areas, they have been highlighted and presented by region. Analytical overviews provide a backdrop against which the narratives are highlighted, leaving the reader to make a collage, rather than draw a conclusion which may, indeed, be counter-intuitive to the spirit of the features.

Within the regions

In Africa, a continent that is rapidly changing, plagued by war, famine, drought and political instability, the level of women organising is astonishing, in spite of the single-party political systems that prevail in most African countries. As is commonly quoted, almost 80 per cent of Africa's agriculture is managed by women and the greatest problem, as the WFS features highlight, lies in the fact that women are not considered to be farmers. In addition, customary law, which is still widely practised, acts as a further deterrent to real equity for African women. While it can be argued, as it has been by African developmentalists, that inequity affects both men and women, its gender-specific implications for women cannot be ignored if real development for women is also to take place. Even in newly independent states such as Namibia, where women played a major role in the struggle for democracy, they have been relegated to less than equal status and have to continuously remind their people and their government of their aspirations and needs. This, despite the fact that Namibia's constitution is among the most egalitarian. In South Africa, which is moving towards majority rule, women have a similar preoccupation and will continue to have to keep their interests in the nation's consciousness, as it emerges.

The Asian region has experienced a great deal of change as well, and diversities and disparities are stark. Countries such as Burma, Pakistan, Nepal, Bangladesh, Russia, Afghanistan, the Philippines, have all undergone major social, economic and political changes. In many of these the environmental agenda has been strongly articulated, and linked directly to poverty and inequity. In Malaysia, Thailand and Indonesia people's movements have come into being, very often after immense degradation has already taken place. In Japan where, since World War II, women have had a low status despite the enormous economic strides made, they have come forward to organise and speak out boldly against the 'economic miracle' and what it has meant for Japanese society. Regional conflicts and war have also had a damaging effect on the environment and on development advances in the region.

In Latin America the decade of the Eighties heralded democratic governments elected by the people, but years of indebtedness have trapped the people and served as an obstacle to the region's progress. Regional conflicts, wars, insurgency and heavy-handed governments have further exacerbated the situation. People's aspirations have been crushed, often brutally, by the military and authoritarian governments. Thousands of people have disappeared in the continent, never to be seen again, lost as a statistic. Women have spoken out, marched, cried and lobbied to get their children and spouses back. And as in Africa and Asia, grassroots communities have begun to see that the only way out of the quagmire is to organise and empower themselves; again, in all three, women are often in the forefront of these movements and community efforts.

In all three regions there are certain common denominators which are either responsible for, or have exacerbated, the environmental crisis. The regional overviews that precede the features spell these out, but what is striking is that each region has been equally affected by the ills of export-led development in the form of balance of payments problems, structural adjustment, and the crippling cost of debt servicing. All regional overviews address the issues of poverty, high birth-rates, migration, falling commodity prices and declining resource flows, neglect of the agriculture sector, and the marginalisation of women — or, as has also been suggested, the feminization of poverty. The reviews also point out how the oppression of people has led to two main responses: migration or agitation.

The overviews also suggest that the governments of the South, democratic or dictatorial, have not kept their promises to the people; indeed, there is plenty of evidence that indicates that they have, instead, aggravated the deteriorating status of people and their environments, through a combination of ill-thought out priorities and insufficient attention to the consequences of western-style development. In all three regions government articulation of environmental issues is relatively recent, often less than a decade old. A major reason for this has been the misapprehension that putting environmental concerns into practice would mean curtailing economic development. Colleen Morna in her overview of Africa gives the example of Cote d'Ivoire, where the government and environmentalists have been at odds over the construction of a road through one of the country's remaining rain-forests; the heavily indebted government argues that it has little choice but to exploit what it has to get out of its economic bind.

Patricia Baeza in her overview of Latin America also draws the link between exploitation of natural resources, such as forests and lands for export, at the expense of local survival. The once fertile north-eastern region of Brazil, which in the 19th century was the sugar capital of the country, is now drought-ridden, overpopulated and poverty stricken, and has resorted to forced sterilisation of women and the killing of street children by death squads.

The push for accelerating the export of commodities can have severe consequences for whole communities. Sujata Madhok gives an example from India when exports of cotton yarn rose from 40 million kgs in 1987-88, to over a 100 million kgs in 1990-91. While this was good news for India's balance of payments situation, thousands of handloom weavers in a country renowned for a centuries old textile tradition were renderd unemployed and destitute. At the end of 1991 in the state of Andhra Pradesh in south India, at least 73 starvation deaths among weavers were reported in the mainstream press in over just two months.

Developing, displacing

Does poverty precede environmental degradation or is it the other way around? In the case of Africa, Colleen Morna shares the best documented case of a Nigerian peasant persuaded by an Italian company in 1987 to store barrels of waste on his farm for $120 a month. Investigations by the local press and then by the government, which brought in the United States Environmental Protection Agency, and British and Japanese atomic agencies, were too late: the peasant died and the village soils and waters were poisoned.

But there are other examples where people and governments are not motivated by poverty but by short-sightedness, greed and callousness; an example is the well-known and well-documented case of Love Canal. In the 1940s, in the city of Niagara Falls, USA, the Hooker Chemical Company first buried 22,000 tons of chemicals; they then sold the property in the 1960s saying it was the most "desirable" location for a school. But then strange things began happening: children were getting sick and burned and pregnant women were aborting spontaneously. It was not until the 1970s that pregnant women and children began to be evacuated from Love Canal. In 1978 President Jimmy Carter declared a national emergency on the adverse impact of chemical wastes lying exposed on the surface, and associated chemical vapours from the Love Canal Chemical Waste Landfill.

Love Canal was not the first or the worst hazardous waste disaster; it was the most famous because of the way the residents organised for justice. The movement started by Lois Gibbs, a home-maker at Love Canal, has evolved as the Citizens Clearinghouse for Hazardous Wastes (CCHW) which celebrates its tenth anniversary in 1992. It has over 7000 local grassroots groups as members and its goal is to build strong community-based organisations to resist the dumping of toxic wastes. It provides organising and technical advice through manuals, over the telephone, and on-site visits.

Probably the greatest tragedy of development in recent decades has been the loss of land that belonged to communities, or common lands, that landless poor depended on for sustenance, for grazing cattle, fuelwood or just space for various occupations. The forests have also been a source of sustenance, providing fuelwood, grass and leaves for fodder, fruits and roots for food, herbs for medicine, wood and bamboo for housing, wild grasses for baskets and ropes. These lands have been encroached upon by village elites and the forests taken over by governments.

Sujata Madhok raises an important issue for Asia, which applies to Africa as well. Governments face international pressure to enforce conservation of forest flora and fauna. These, and the demands of tourism, have prompted many governments and conservationists to declare certain areas as 'sanctuaries', off limits to forest-dwellers who may be their original inhabitants. It is paradoxical that the life of a tiger or elephant is valued over human life in such instances and, pitted against the environment that they are an inherent part of, communities are sometimes forced into violent resistance. Several years ago, villagers who were denied access to the Bharatpur Bird Sanctuary in northern India set part of it on fire, in protest.

A critical reading of the material suggests that displacement is an overwhelming theme. Just as the challenges before women farmers are formidable, the plight of women who have migrated to the urban areas becomes equally compelling. Just the sheer number of women that have moved from a land based economy to an urban, market-oriented one, is staggering. While governments blithely talk of the family as a norm, more and more households are headed by women and even more children roam the streets, either abandoned by their parents or runaways from home. The discrimination in defining women as appendages to men is clear in terms of land

policy, where women cannot inherit land or have no rights to
it once their spouses die. Overnight, women are displaced,
thrown out of their homes and communities, or forced to
become wage labourers.

The rapid move from the rural to the urban areas also
highlights the change in rural economy when women stop
subsistence farming and either switch to cash cropping (more
incentives) or move to urban areas where they become traders.
The effect of these shifts on health, nutrition, and so on, has
been well-documented over the years. Since most incentives
for women in rural communities are in the area of income
generation, often for goods and services that earn them
income, they generally lead to a change of life-style that could
well be unsustainable.

The power to change

Sustainable life-styles, or the search for them, is a strong theme
of many of the features that appear in the book. The WFS
insistence on primary evidence resulted in a kind of introspection and sharing that allows an in-depth look at the intimate,
and not-so-intimate, concerns of people and situations being
written about. Beginning with the people themselves, the
features make the connection between a problem, its causes,
its solution and the possibilities of change, and presents
people's perceptions of what is valid for them. For example,
in Chapare, Bolivia, a traditional cocoa-growing area, local
farmers insist that their coca is not cocaine, citing centuries of
use of coca for health and nutritional reasons. It is cocaine, they
argue, for commercial traders and cocaine addicts. The
activism on the part of the growers results from their consciousness about the relationship between increasing poverty
in the region and the use of the crop as an income generation
substance.

Similarly, in Kenya and Zimbabwe, communities are re-
searching and recommending the use of insects in daily diets
to overcome nutritional problems and to preserve high-risk
pests (which is what they become) such as locusts. Tradition-

ally, insects were a part of the family diet, mixed with sauces and eaten as a snack or a main meal. The communities feel these traditions should be revived in the interest of balanced policies for nutritional and environmental concerns.

In the Philippines, an environmental activist, tired of waiting for the government to act decisively on the worsening depletion of the Philippine forests, filed a suit on behalf of 39 children, three of whom were his own. All the children were under 17. At issue was the debate over logging, where trees were being cut at the rate of 150,000-200,000 hectares a year. According to the lawyer, by the time his three-year old became 15, there would be no forests left.

These three examples are a reflection of what other features suggest: a macro view of development from the micro level. As such they represent and give a voice to the values, aspirations and opinions of millions in the South who talk about development as they experience it. In fine-tuning this material for publication, we have tried to put it in a wider context so that connections can be made. Sometimes, prominent or well-known campaigns have been set aside to make place for others, as important, but not nearly as familiar. Thus, the Chipko Andolan (movement) of India or the Greenbelt Movement of Kenya, revolutionary in their own way, have been featured here at an angle, so to speak, to reveal the process behind the change, rather then the event itself, or a particular person or organisation.

As the book is being prepared it is the sixth anniversary of the Chernobyl nuclear disaster, in which explosion and fire at the plant on April 26, 1986, sent a radioactive cloud over large areas of Europe. At that time, only 31 people were officially reported to have died in the accident; six years later, Urkrainian officials held a press conference stating that between 6000 and 8000 Ukrainians died in the aftermath. At roughly the same time, a significant decision was handed down in India in the Bhopal gas leak case when the judge ordered immediate attachment of all movable and immovable properties of the multinational Union Carbide Corporation of India. This was with reference to an on-going controversy that stemmed from a poisonous (MIC) gas leak in December 1984, which killed and maimed several thousand Indians.

While history repeats itself with such industrial disasters, Love Canal, Chernobyl and Bhopal are worth mentioning because they epitomise the inability of governments to be above-board about their agendas. Even as human lives are being lost, mangled and betrayed, governments continue to lie, manipulate and distort the truth, without accepting responsibility for their citizens. Chernobyl and Bhopal, like Love Canal in the US, are but three examples of such tragedies. Other development projects, such as giant dams in all parts of the world, have brought about a tremendous displacement of people, a fact that governments and international organisations, in the name of development, have explained away as the price to pay for progress. Export-oriented development policies have created an economic climate in which local needs have taken a back seat and the emphasis is on the production of goods and services for an external market. While export is essential for any country, the attempt of many nations of the South to build their economies on the demands of an external market have taken a heavy toll on workers; various features in the book make direct or indirect references to the changes in the lives of workers, increasingly displaced from their professions, skills and work rights.

The fact that a middle class of entrepreneurs is achieving a standard of living on the backs of working class people is neither new nor revealing. What is disturbing is that in spite of economic growth and productivity, inequity continues to rise. And it is this inequity that will not allow sustainable development to take place: for all the trees planted, industrial pollutants reduced or banned, environment friendly products introduced, appropriate technology adopted and aid levels increased, the causes will have to be ruthlessly addressed. The countries of the South are caught in a bind, or so it would seem, in a heavy dependence on aid and trade with the countries of the North, so much so that the South feels it cannot solve its problems without this equation. If this is true, as the features suggest, then the South needs to come up with alternatives for creating a situation in which the equation can change. At present, this is not happening. Restructuring of many of the southern economies is based on the International Monetary Fund model of development, of which export-led growth is a cornerstone. Very few countries of the South have been able to come out clean from such contracts; what is more, they feel they have no other recourse.

Recourse or not, development models currently undertaken in the South have created an environment in which a climate of struggle has evolved. This struggle is based on people's perceptions of what is needed to change their lives; whether it is issue-, gender-, race- or class-based it provides a powerful voice for the need to create an alternative development. It then becomes the task of the international community, individual governments, regional coalitions, non-governmental organisations to listen and learn.

Too often, the marginalised are considered powerless, faceless, invisible and second class, especially when they happen to be women. We feel that women and the disenfranchised are none of these, that, indeed the periphery matters, and that change is possible. The book stresses this by presenting narratives that show that people want, are willing to struggle for, and have the power to change.

Anita Anand

Africa

FROM THE EXPANDING edges of the Sahara desert to the gulleys that dissect Lesotho like gaping wounds, and the red rivers that bleed out of Madagascar into the Indian Ocean, an aerial overview of Africa tells the same story. The poet's dream of a vast, wooded landscape where nature dances to the setting sun is no more: stripped of its trees and grass, Africa is being drained of its lifeline — the soil — faster than anywhere else in the world.

By the early 1980s Africa had 37 per cent of the world's drylands, and the situation is fast deteriorating. In a survey undertaken by the United Nations Sudano Sahelian office in 1989, half the respondents reported significantly worse conditions of drought and desertification. At the current rate, the United Nations warns, soil erosion could lower agricultural output in Africa by 25 per cent over the 1975-2000 period.

At the root of this potential holocaust is poverty, which has become both the cause and consequence of a vicious circle of degradation. Poverty is partly a consequence of internal factors, such as inappropriate policies, especially the neglect of agriculture and the crucial role that women play in it; failure to halt population growth, corruption, mismanagement and war; and partly it has been caused by external forces, including colonialism, continued inequities in the world economic order, mounting debt and externally imposed structural adjustment programmes.

The Nineties have opened with commodity prices still on their downard spiral, few signs of a more equitable global trade system emerging, as yet no durable solution to the debt problem, a new preoccupation in the west with eastern Europe, and a reluctance to unequivocally commit itself to reducing the gap between rich and poor. Natural calamities, like the devastating drought in southern Africa, and the killer disease AIDS now ravaging the continent, have added to the bleak picture, so often portrayed in the western media, of a continent beyond redemption. The lost decade of the Eighties, many fear, is now set to repeat itself in the Nineties, with even more alarming consequences for the environment.

Yet planted in this desert of doom are blossoms of hope. The disasters of the Eighties have prompted an unprecedented introspection by both governments and donors. A new consensus is emerging that while it is important to correct macro-economic ills, development in Africa cannot be sustained unless it involves, and addresses the needs of, the people at a grassroots level who are both the subject and object of economic reform. Agriculture, including land reform, the provision of credit, extension, and marketing facilities — with a particular emphasis on the needs of women, and of adopting environmentally sustainable strategies — are beginning to occupy their rightful place in development planning. With the ending of the Cold War and political changes in South Africa, some of the continent's worst wars, and greatest contributors to poverty and degradation, are winding down.

Moves toward democracy in eastern Europe, coupled with mounting internal pressure, have witnessed some of the first transfers of power through the ballot box in Africa. Today, virtually every one of the continent's 53 countries has been touched in some way by the clamour for political pluralism, and more democratic and transparent government.

All these factors — cumulatively referred to by the World Bank and others as an "enabling environment" — bode well for the emergence in Africa of grassroots movements which, literally and figuratively, are the continent's best hope for holding back the desert. Already, there are numerous examples of organisations that have challenged policies designed to derive short term economic benefit at the expense of longer term environmental damage. Many, with limited resources, and few tools other than their bare hands, are working to reverse the damage that has already been caused.

As in so many other local initiatives in Africa, women are invariably taking the lead. Like the soil which nurtures new plant life, they give birth to, and feed Africa's children. The fate of both are intimately linked. As Kenyan environmentalist Wangari Maathai, referring to the Greenbelt Movement of women planting trees across Kenya, puts it in one of the WFS features in this series: "We work together to conserve what remains of our environment."

What went wrong ?

To begin with, although Africa is well endowed with natural resources, these are delicately balanced. The continent straddles tropical and sub-tropical zones where, by virtue of the climate, environmental conditions are more fragile than in temperate regions. As Paul Harrison, author of *The Greening of Africa* writes: "Most African soils are infertile and bad at holding water or nutrients. The best soils are found in valley bottoms, where they are prone to waterlogging, or on volcanic hills, where erosion is a problem. The climate is harsh, dry or unpredictable over vast areas. Dry spells come along at any time, withering crops. Two-thirds of the continent can expect droughts of at least two years' duration every fifty years."

Traditionally, Africans practised a system of shifting cultivation in which, after tilling a piece of land for three to four years, farmers moved on, leaving the original land to regain its fertility during fallow periods of up to twenty years. During the colonial era, however, large tracts of land were turned over to plantations, reducing the land available to peasant farmers. The effects are especially marked in southern Africa, where some colonisers settled permanently; in Zimbabwe, half of the country's best land was legally reserved for whites, who comprised three per cent of the population, while in Namibia 65 per cent of the land was designated for the country's six per cent white population. South Africa's 87 per cent indigenous population has been forced into ethnic reserves covering a barren 13 per cent of the land surface.

Rapid population growth has exacerbated the problem of inequitable land distribution. Unlike most prosperous countries, where population growth rates are falling, the growth rate in Africa, where children are seen as a source of economic security, stands at three per cent: the highest in the world. Africa's population has more than doubled since 1950, to 500 million, and by the end of the century there will be 877 million mouths to feed. Where land was once left to regenerate its fertility, trees are being ruthlessly cut down. According to a World Bank briefing paper titled *Population, Agriculture and Environment*, in 1980, "Sub-Saharan Africa had about 660 million hectares of forest and woodland. About 3.2 million hectares has been lost each year since. New forests have been planted at the rate of only about 90,000 hectares a year. Since 1965, Togo's forests have shrunk from 45 per cent of its total land area to 25 per cent; Malawi's from 54 per cent to 46 per cent; Uganda's from 32 per cent to 29 per cent."

The effects are evident in dwindling supplies of firewood, soil erosion and a loss of 63 per cent of the continent's original wildlife habitat. Humans have similarly encroached on pasture lands. In many parts of Africa, overgrazing has reduced grass cover so low that large gulleys, or dongas, as they are called in southern Africa, criss-cross the landscape.

Farm sizes are also shrinking. According to the World Bank, the amount of arable land available per person has declined from an average 0.5 hectares in 1965 to 0.3 hectares in 1987. This reflects in the reduced size of household farms; in Tanzania, for example, farms in the Arusha area have shrunk from five to 1.5 hectares; and in Malawi, a quarter of rural households have less than one hectare of land.

The combined effect of new patterns of land tenure and population growth is that the system of shifting cultivation has now been abandoned. A more settled form of agriculture is theoretically sustainable, with the agricultural practices and inputs that ensure that the soil maintains its fertility. In most African countries, this has not been the case.

Neglect of the agricultural sector

During the colonial era, policies deliberately discriminated against small scale farmers, and in favour of large plantations; infrastructure, finance and extension services were designed to service the latter. Where government extension workers reached peasant farmers, they were viewed with suspicion, often forcing peasant farmers to dig contour ridges under threat of imprisonment.

When most African countries gained independence from British, French and Portuguese colonial rulers between 1957 and 1965, they invariably saw rapid industrialisation as the quickest route to development. Thus, for example, a country like Zambia, with huge agricultural potential, concentrated all its energies on mining copper, only to fall on hard times when prices of this metal fell. Overvalued exchange rates made export crops less competitive. To hold down urban food costs, farmers received pitiful prices, while inefficient state-owned agricultural marketing authorities further whittled away farmers' profits.

Following on from the colonial period, many African governments discouraged positive traditional practices, such as intercropping, which keeps pests and weeds down and reduces the risk of losing everything in a bad year. Considerable emphasis has been put on chemical fertilisers which are often too expensive for peasant farmers, and can have harmful environmental effects. Chemical pesticides, by killing natural enemies along with the pests, have often led to a resurgence of these pests in greater numbers. Multinational companies, by continuing to sell to Africa pesticides long banned in the west, such as DDT, have not helped matters, and aid agencies have fuelled the problem. In Zimbabwe, for example, the EEC has funded a project to eradicate the tsetse fly, which causes sleeping sickness in cattle, in the ecologically fragile Zambezi Valley. This has obvious benefits for the cattle and those who own them; on the other hand, the project has been strongly criticised by environmentalists because of the use of chemical sprays, and the danger to the area of an influx of human settlers.

Governments and aid agencies, writes Paul Harrison, "came along with technologies developed in Europe, America or Asia and tried to impose them. They brought tractors that damaged the soil, improved plant varieties that did worse than local varieties, fertilisers that lost money in dry years. Thus, many development projects failed, and it is the farmers who paid the price."

According to the UN Food and Agriculture Organisation (FAO), in 1938 Africa exported cereals; in 1950 Africa was self-sufficient; in 1976 Africa imported ten million tonnes of cereals; in 1978, 13 million tonnes and in 1983, 31 million tonnes. Unable to earn a living from the land, peasant farmers in African countries have been forced to seek work on commercial farms, in mines, and in towns. For countries neighbouring South Africa, often the most lucrative option has been to go and work in the huge South African gold mines. In the case of Lesotho, which is completely surrounded by South Africa, the payment by the South African government of heavy subsidies to white commercial farmers in the neighbouring Transvaal province, made it cheaper for the country to buy food from its neighbour than for peasant farmers themselves to produce it. Today, more than half of the country's foreign exchange earnings are derived from the remittances of migrant workers. With 70 per cent of its people living in towns, South Africa has the highest rate of urbanisation, followed by Zambia, which has a 50 per cent rate of urbanisation because of its mining-based economy.

The average for the continent is 30 per cent — still the lowest in the world. However, according to the UN Population Fund (UNFPA) this figure is growing by five per cent each year. At this rate, in another thirty years or so, more Africans will live in cities than in the countryside. The figure is especially worrying when one considers that unemployment in most African countries runs at anything between 30 and 50 per cent.

The marginalisation of women

A particular feature of urbanisation in Africa is that often it involves young men migrating to towns, leaving women, who are already burdened with huge domestic responsibilities, to do the farming as well. Unemployment is markedly higher among those women who do follow their husbands to towns than among men, leaving most to earn a living in the so-called "informal sector" where hours are long and returns low. UN figures show that with an average working week of over 65 hours, African women are second only to those of eastern Europe in the length of their working week, if unpaid domestic work is taken into account. The gap between this, and the average hours worked by African men, is also one of the widest — some 12 to 13 hours a week.

One in five African households has a woman as its head, even though more often than not they do not have title to land, or family possessions. In southern Africa, where migrant labour is even more predominant, the figure is higher; in Botswana, for example, almost one in two households is headed by a female. Yet policies designed to improve agriculture have consistently ignored the fact that 80 per cent of producers in Africa are women. According to a United Nations briefing paper, only two to ten per cent of the outreach of agricultural extension schemes is directed at women; credit schemes, and other centralised efforts to improve agriculture have generally tended to ignore them.

Women, children, food security, and the environment, have also been the main victims of the over twenty wars that have killed seven million people, and created five million refugees on the continent during the last two decades. Ill-conceived colonial boundaries, cutting through ethnic groups, and throwing others together, have aggravated many of these conflicts (for example the Nigerian civil war, the incessant wars in Chad, conflicts in Sudan, the secessionist movement in Eritrea, and current faction-fighting in Liberia.) Border disputes have also sparked wars between countries: Somalia and Kenya; Ethiopia and Somalia; Libya and Chad; Mali and Burkina Faso, to take just a few examples.

As country by country abandoned political pluralism, muzzled the press and clamped down on human rights, military coups became the only way to express dissent. Since the Sixties, Africa has experienced no less than 40 coups, with many of the coup leaders proving as corrupt and inept as those whom they heroically overthrew. The continent has also witnessed second generation liberation wars, in Uganda, Ethiopia and Somalia. Until recently, the Cold War fanned the flames of virtually every conflict in Africa, most pronounced in Angola, and the Horn.

In southern Africa, protracted independence wars were waged in Mozambique, Angola, Namibia, and Zimbabwe, while an internal guerilla war and mass protests have continued in South Africa. The latter also engaged in numerous acts of destabilisation against its neighbours, estimated by the United Nations to have cost the region $60 billion in direct damage and lost revenues. Much of this resulted from South Africa's covert and overt support for UNITA rebels in Angola, and Renamo rebels in Mozambique. The cost in human and environmental terms is even more devastating. In Mozambique, for example, almost one-third of the country's 14 million people have either been internally displaced or forced to flee the country as refugees.

Around Maputo, Mozambique's capital, the deforested fuelwood ring is 55 kms wide. Those remaining in the countryside, or in refugee camps in neighbouring countries, have similarly, in the struggle for survival, stripped the soil bare. Wildlife populations have also been decimated, not least by rebels who have funded much of their brutal war through the illegal sale of ivory. *Greenwar,* a book by Sahelian writers, traces the insidious relationship between war, poverty and degradation in this belt of Africa. It concludes:

> The cycle of impoverishment is repetitive and truly vicious. Environmental impoverishment, increasing conflict over resources, marginalisation of rural people, social and political unrest, displacement and uncontrolled migration lead to further conflict and the outbreak of wars within and between states. When hostilities grow into organised warfare, the environment inevitably undergoes further degradation. This insidious pattern

comes full circle, as a peacetime population and the government struggle to cope with a land left environmentally bankrupt. The seeds are sown for further tension and conflict.

Falling commodity prices, declining resource flows

External forces, apart from fuelling many of the conflicts in Africa, have exacerbated poverty and environmental degradation. During the 1970s commodity prices were buoyant. Disaster struck in the 1980s when major changes in international markets, including moves toward synthetic inputs and recession, led to a sharp decline. According to *Africa Recovery,* a quarterly published by the United Nations Development Programme (UNDP), in volume terms Africa's exports grew by an average of 2.5 per cent since 1986, yet the unit value of these exports fell to two-thirds the level that prevailed in 1980. Concurrently, the unit value of Africa's imports increased, compared with 1980. As a result, the purchasing power of a given amount of African exports had fallen by nearly half by 1990.

Crops most severely affected include cocoa and coffee, a major export of 15 or more African countries. Between 1985 and 1989, according to the UN, African cocoa producers lost over three billion dollars, despite a 26 per cent jump in output. Oil exporting countries have also been badly hit by the slump in oil prices, about half what they were from 1986 to 1990, as for the preceding five years. Meanwhile, co-operation on international commodity issues has, according to *Africa Recovery,* "fallen to its lowest point since the Sixties". Coffee, cocoa, and tin agreements, designed to stabilise the prices of these international commodities, have collapsed.

Africa has lost $50 billion as a result of falling commodity prices since 1986 — far more than has been given in aid — while protectionism in northern markets has made it difficult to expand exports. Although some donors substantially increased aid to Africa, net resource flows declined, from 24.6 billion in 1986 to 23.3 billion in 1990.

Debt

During the commodity boom of the Seventies, many African governments, with the willing support of donors, banks and multilateral agencies, borrowed lavishly to finance large scale (and often white elephant) development projects. Falling commodity prices, coupled with high interest, and volatile exchange rate movements throughout the Eighties in creditor countries have contributed to mounting debt problems.

Africa's indebtedness, according to World Bank figures, has ballooned from $140 billion in 1982, to $272 billion in 1990. This is equivalent to 90 per cent of the continent's and 112 per cent of sub-Saharan Africa's Gross Domestic Product, compared to equivalent figures of 48 per cent in Latin America, and 50 per cent in eastern Europe. Debt service, at $20 billion annually, chews up 30 per cent of export earnings, achieved through import compression and cutbacks on investment.

Even so, many countries are not meeting their full obligations. For example Nigeria, which has a debt of $34 billion, would require $5.56 billion to service its debt this year, but has decided that it will pay no more than $2.5 billion, or 30 per cent of export earnings, to its creditors. If Tanzania met its full debt service bill, this would amount to a staggering 94 per cent of export earnings, with 49 per cent of that going into interest payments alone.

Mounting arrears have forced a growing realisation that the current situation is not sustainable. Because 42 per cent of Africa's debt is owed to bilateral creditors, reducing official debt — which includes concessional and non-concessional aid — has been the primary concern. Some progress has been made in reducing concessional debt owed by Africa's poorest countries. In 1987, the World Bank and 18 other multilateral and bilateral donors launched the Special Programme of Assistance (SPA) for the 23 African countries eligible for low interest aid from the bank's International Development Agency (IDA) and undertaking structural adjustment programmes. The aim of the project has been to increase resource flows to these countries through a combination of debt relief and new money.

Between 1978 and 1990, according to the World Bank, donors cancelled some $7.8 billion in official development assistance owed by SPA countries. Additional cancellations recently announced by France, the USA and Italy will substantially reduce the remaining $2 billion concessional debt owed by the poorest African countries. This still leaves $7 billion owed by low income African countries to donors not from the Organisation for Economic Cooperation and Development (OECD), principally in eastern Europe and the Middle East, representing particular problems for some countries, especially those that had close links with the former Soviet Union.

For OECD countries, forgiveness of concessional debt is important insofar as it represents an acknowledgement of the principle of cancellation, rather than rescheduling. However, since much of this money was not being paid anyway, and carries low interest rates, the short term cash flow benefits for debtor countries is minimal, accounting for a reduction of debt service payments of $100 million annually.

Of more critical importance is the non-concessional debt owed by African countries to donors and dealt with through the Paris Club. Many donors have now accepted the so-called Toronto terms which provide three options: forgive one-third of debt service due; reschedule with longer grace periods; and reschedule at lower interest rates. However, most have yet to accept the more far reaching Trinidad terms, proposed by British Prime Minister John Major, then Chancellor of the Exchequer, to increase the amount to be written off to two-thirds.

Even then, the debt burden would not be sustainable for many of the poorest countries. This recognition underpins the more radical proposal made by the United Nations Secretary General during a review in late 1991, of the five year UN Programme of Action for African Economic Recovery and Development (UNPAAERD), for a cancellation of all the official debt.

However, mainly at the insistence of the US (which has resisted cancelling non-concessional aid on technical grounds, and any attempt at across the board solutions to African debt on political grounds) the UN resolution called for a "case by case" application of measures "going well beyond the relief granted under the Toronto terms" for the poorest, most indebted countries. A crucial, outstanding issue for Africa is its lower middle income countries which — unlike counterparts in the Third World — are largely indebted to official, rather than commercial creditors, and face serious payment problems despite their status. Between 1987 and 1989, according to World Bank figures, these countries received a mere $206 million in concessional aid cancelled, and have largely remained outside the Toronto agreement.

Because commercial debt is relatively insignificant for most African countries, the Brady initiative, helpful in reducing Latin America's debt, has only been applied in Morocco. Market-based solutions to commercial debt, such as debt-equity, and debt for nature swaps, have also necessarily been more limited than in Latin America, although some innovative schemes have been hatched. For example, in August 1991, the World Wildlife Fund bought the title to US $2.1 million of Madagascar's debt through US Bankers Trust Company at a discount of 45 per cent. The WWF received this amount in local currency, being invested in two national parks.

The World Bank has established a $100 million Debt Reduction Facility to provide $10 million to low income countries to buy back their commercial debt, but it is estimated that $500 million is needed. Despite spearheading debt initiatives, the multilateral agencies do not reschedule debt themselves, and monies owed to them (accounting for over a third of Africa's debt) present a major headache for low and middle income African countries. Some assistance has been forthcoming from donors to help countries in arrears with the Bank and Fund. However, a recommendation by the UN Secretary General that ways be found to substantially reduce Africa's multilateral debt met with stiff resistance from western donors, especially the US, on the basis that such action would undermine the credit ratings of the multilateral institutions.

Thus the overall picture with regard to Africa's debt is that while the principle of reducing the debt stock has now been accepted, questions of magnitude, and eligibility of debt carrying market interest rates, especially non-concessional aid and multilateral debt, still loom large. Substantial debt cancellations by the US for Egypt and Poland, largely on political grounds, shows that with the requisite political will, the debt issue can be resolved. For Africa as a whole, this is still not the case. As Zimbabwe's Finance Minister, Bernard Chidzero, a former chairman of the World Bank's Development Committee puts it: "We need a durable, effective debt strategy under which no country should ever have to pay or meet its debt service obligations at the expense of growth."

Structural adjustment

The quid pro quo for aid and debt relief in African countries is that they undertake economic structural adjustment programmes, agreed to with (or more often dictated by) the IMF and World Bank. Over thirty countries have now undertaken these programmes which include devaluation to make exports more competitive; removing price controls, cutting of subsidies and social expenditure, privatisation of parastatals, and the trimming of civil services.

Some of these policies have been beneficial. For example, the removal of price controls, and privatisation of state marketing agencies has improved the returns to farmers; however, real improvement has often continued to be undermined by poor infrastructure. The rising costs of imported inputs, and the removal of subsidies on such items as fertiliser have also often proved to be counter-productive. In Lesotho, officials complain that IMF and World Bank insistence on removing subsidies has made it impossible for their farmers to ever be able to compete against South African counterparts, making farming, and with it better land management, even more unattractive.

Structural adjustment, it is now generally agreed, has tended to exacerbate poverty. For those who depend on buying food — either those who do not produce enough to feed themselves in the rural areas, or urban dwellers — the removal of price controls has sent food prices soaring. Nowhere has this been more painfully evident than in Zambia which, because of its large urban population, has witnessed recurrent unrest over food costs. Cuts in social spending have affected the poor disproportionately, because they do not have the resources to obtain these facilities privately. According to the UNPAAERD review: "The percentage of total government expenditure devoted to health in 1985 was nearly six per cent and to education 15 per cent. By 1990, the share of health and education in total government expenditure had declined to five and 11 per cent respectively." Cuts in health spending slowed progress in reducing infant mortality and maternal mortality rates, both the highest in the world. Although literacy rates increased, the total number of illiterates has been rising. Primary school enrolments have fallen from 77 per cent in 1980 to 70 per cent in 1990.

Thousands, especially in the lowest paid categories, have lost their jobs, while all those in the wage earning sector have experienced a decline in real wages of over 30 per cent in the 1980s, making most Africans today poorer than at independence in the 1960s. Disease, poor sanitation, inadequate housing and squalor, have aggravated environmental degradation in Africa's cities.

Unemployment and insufficient wages have led to a blossoming of the informal sector, often dominated by women. While it has shown immense creativity, it too has often been driven to a callous attitude toward the environment, such as stripping wood around major cities for sale as firewood. In Nigeria and other countries, the removal of subsidies on kerosene has made for an increase in the use of wood for fuel in urban areas.

In the west, adopting more environmentally sound practices involves a slight lowering of living standards; in Africa, the allocation of resources is a life and death issue. This explains why, in a study carried out by the United Nations Environment Programme (UNEP) recently, the majority of African respondents agreed wholeheartedly with the assertion: "Life in this country is so difficult today that what's happening to the environment is not of much concern." Herbert Acquay, an

African Resource Policy Analyst at Cornell University says, "The average person in Africa is too preoccupied with finding decent shelter, adequate nutrition, health care and education for his/her family to worry about saving an elephant or a forest."

The drive to increase exports, and the push to achieve growth at all costs explains the dilemmas that governments face as they make choices between immediate economic gain, and longer term environmental degradation. In Cote d' Ivoire, for example, the government and environmentalists have been at odds over the construction of a road through one of the country's few remaining rain-forests, and along highly vulnerable ecosystems of lagoons and mangrove forest which fulfil functions like providing an interface between the Atlantic and tropical rain-forests. With only 1.5 m ha of the 12 m ha of rain-forest it had in the 1970s left, Cote d'Ivoire has suffered one of the highest rates of deforestation in the world. But, as a heavily indebted, lower middle African country largely dependent on cocoa, it argues that it has little choice but to expolit what it has to get out of the current quagmire.

Next door in Ghana, which has lost 80 per cent of its forest cover, the government recently admitted that it is still exporting charcoal to Britain and the Middle East. Indeed, this product is one of 88 non-traditional exports registered by the Ghana Export Promotion Council. The Council was set up under the country's decade old economic structural adjustment programme to help reduce Ghana's dependence on cocoa exports.

One of the most telling illustrations of how poverty has driven people and countries to environmental damage is the dumping of toxic wastes in Africa. Possibly the best documented case was that of a Nigerian peasant farmer persuaded by an Italian company in 1987 to store barrels of such wastes on his farm for $120 a month. Investigations by the local press, and then by the government, which brought in the United States Environmental Protection Agency, and United Kingdom and Japanese atomic agencies, proved too late. The farmer died, the village soil and waters were poisoned.

African governments, under the Organisation of African Unity have now signed the "Bamako Convention on the Ban of the Import into Africa and the Control of Transboundary Movement and Management Within Africa of Hazardous Wastes" — the world's most comprehensive toxic import ban. But reticence by western countries to formalise a similar worldwide ban in the run-up to the Earth Summit in 1992, and documents leaked from the World Bank suggesting that storing toxic wastes might be a good way for Africans to earn money, are a source of serious concern.

Outlook for the Nineties

The efficacy of structural adjustment programmes has been the subject of considerable debate between the World Bank — which argues that countries undertaking adjustment are doing better than those that are not — and the UN Economic Commission for Africa, which has disputed the World Bank figures. The overall trend, in any case, is not encouraging. According to the UN Secretary General's UNPAAERD review, Africa's economic output in the years 1986 and 1990 grew by 2.3 per cent in real terms, well below the rate of population growth, meaning on average, the GDP fell by 0.7 per cent.

In his report, the Secretary General estimated that to double the continent's annual per capita income to the modest sum of $700, Africa would have to achieve an annual growth rate of six per cent per annum over the next 24 years. This would require $30 billion in net official development assistance by 1992, to increase on a cumulative basis at four per cent per annum till the year 2000. Debate in the General Assembly on Africa's economic recovery was, however, marked by a tough attitude on the part of western governments, who blamed African governments for their internal shortcomings, while Africa blamed the west for its preoccupation with eastern Europe. In the ultimate *New Agenda for the Development of Africa in the 1990s,* western donors committed themselves to "provide additional resource flows to Africa that will complement domestic efforts and financial resources" without putting a figure to this support. As noted under the section on debt, donors further rejected outright cancellation of official debt, and agreed only to a feasibility study on an African Diversification Fund, aimed to help Africa reduce its current dependence on single commodities.

The divergence between Africa and the west has similarly been evident in the preparation for the Earth Summit. Efforts by Africans to get poverty placed squarely on the agenda have run into opposition, primarily from the US. The gulf in perceptions between the developing countries of Africa, and industrialised countries over environmental issues is exemplified by the ongoing debate between western and southern African countries over the ivory ban. Southern African countries, who maintain that they have an over-abundance of elephants, often seen as pests by peasant farmers, say the best way to ensure the survival of this species is to give it an economic value by allowing the sale of ivory. Asked by a western journalist if she had no qualms about wearing an ivory necklace, Victoria Chitepo, then Zimbabwe's environment minister, asked him if he didn't feel guilty about wearing shoes.

Ominously, while the west worries about endangered species in Africa, its own pollution-happy policies are leading to global warming, likely to greatly compound Africa's poverty. Many scientists believe that the recent, more severe than usual droughts that Africa has been experiencing are related to global climatic changes. The worst is the one currently being experienced in southern Africa. Normally, in aggregate, a food surplus region, southern Africa currently faces a ten million tonne shortfall of food. The cost of transportation, lost export, and increased import costs are likely to set back by years efforts by many countries in the region to restructure their economies. The United Nations estimates that, all told, 32 million Africans are in danger of famine this year. The World Bank, meanwhile, forecasts growth of 3.5 per cent over the next decade, barely above population growth rate.

Hovering menacingly in the background of any attempts to make accurate forecasts for the region is the rabid spread of AIDS. Proven to thrive in conditions of poverty, the AIDS virus now afflicts six million Africans. Some 800,000 have already developed the disease, half of these women, the highest such percentage in the world. Many children have lost both parents, as graphically illustrated in the story in this series on AIDS orphans in Uganda. AIDS is also claiming Africa's youngest and most economically able, with incalculable consequences on faltering economies and their environments.

Summing up the continent's predicament at the start of the decade, the UNDP's *Africa Recovery,* noted:

> When UNPAAERD was launched, Africa was just emerging from a period of drought, bushfires, famine and food shortages which affected the continent. Civil strife, however, continued to generate huge numbers of refugees and displaced people, putting additional strain on resources. With the return of widespread shortage of rain in 1990, and projected increase in poverty during the 1990s, Africa is facing long term problems for its people and its environment.

Towards a better understanding

Yet amid the gloom, there are glimmers of hope. An upshot of the debate between the World Bank, ECA and UNICEF on the efficacy of structural adjustment was the publication by the World Bank, in 1989, of its ground-breaking report, *Sub-Saharan Africa: From Crisis to Sustainable Growth,* the Bank's most introspective look yet at what has gone wrong with past approaches. Putting forward its theme "adjustment with a difference" the World Bank notes: "Structural adjustment is necessary, but it must be sustained without dogmatism. It must be adjustment with a difference. Difference in the sense that greater accountability is taken of its social impact." Repeatedly referring to the need for greater "capacity building," the report puts a new emphasis on human resource development, environmental protection, and self-reliance. The watchword throughout is on strengthening Africa's capacity to deal with its own problems.

African governments, too, are increasingly taking matters

into their own hands. In 1985, launching Africa's Priority Programme for Economic Recovery 1986 to 1990 (APPER, later complemented by UNPAAERD) African governments reaffirmed that the development of their continent was primarily the responsibility of their governments and their people.

Although the short term prospects are not encouraging, never before has there been a greater consensus on what needs to be done to ensure long term, sustainable, development for Africa. The main aspects of this may be summarised as follows:

Adjustment with a human face: the phrase, coined by UNICEF, is now generally accepted in development circles. Most countries have social security components in their structural adjustment programmes, beginning with Ghana's Programme of Action to Mitigate the Social Costs of Adjustment (PAMSCAD). These include food for work programmes, and provision of basic education and health needs to the poorest segments of society.

Agriculture as a priority: a bright billboard in Ghana, declaring "We Must Eat What We Grow and Grow What We Eat" underscores the almost universal agreement among governments and donors that agriculture must be given priority. Today, 24 African countries have achieved the target, set by APPER, of allocating 20 to 25 per cent of total public investment to agriculture. Zimbabwe, which at independence in 1980 made a concerted effort to encourage small scale farming through the provision of credit, extension services, and marketing arrangements, has proven how versatile and productive peasant farmers can be under the right conditions. Several other countries which had become food deficit areas, such as Zambia and Tanzania, have now become food self-sufficient — bar a drought year.

Women: though still suffering traditional and legal discrimination, they are beginning to receive due recognition as the continent's prime producers and caretakers.

At a UN sponsored conference on the priorities of women in Africa in the 1990s held in Abuja, Nigeria, President Ibrahim Babangida declared, "No national development will be mean-

ingful without the full involvement of women in the development process." According to the UN: "Nearly 80 per cent of
countries have taken specific measures to enhance the role of
women in development. Nineteen countries have reported
positive results from the creation of government departments
and units of women's affairs, new legislation assisting women
and the growing involvement of women in politics." Female
enrolment in primary schools is now almost equal to that of
boys. Some countries have given women legal rights formerly
enjoyed only by men, such as the right to own land and the
right to earn equal pay for equal work. Targets for the year 2000
agreed to by women at the conference included: parity for
women in literacy and primary school education; women
filling one out of five vacant professional government posts;
the signing and ratification by all African countries of the UN
Convention on the Elimination of All Forms of Discrimination
Against Women. So far, only about half of all African countries
have signed the Convention, which was adopted by the
General Assembly in 1979.

Population: according to the UNFPA, all African countries,
except Djibouti, Equatorial Guinea, Gabon, Libya and Somalia
have established mother and child health and family planning
programmes aimed at reducing maternal and infant mortality
rates. Nineteen African countries have programmes designed
to reduce fertility rates as part of their development plans.
There is a deeper understanding that the disadvantaged position of women with respect to employment, access to resources, and decision making is a major obstacle to the reduction
of fertility. Furthermore, there is a recognition by governments
and donors of the paradoxical relationship between poverty
and population: in other words, the poorer the people are, the
more children they will have, and the more difficult it will be
for the environment to support them. The majority of governments have taken measures to try and reduce migration to
urban areas. Zimbabwe, for example, has set up "growth
points" in rural areas, and worked hard to improve rural incomes, to try and stem the tide of migration to the towns.

Environmental issues: both in their immediate and broader

contexts, these are beginning to feature ever more prominently in development plans. African countries, as stated in their Abidjan Declaration, or Common Position to the UNCED, emphasise "the legitimate right of African countries to exploit their natural resources for development purposes". They further stress that "activities to protect the environment should not frustrate the development process". However, the Common Position also underlines that it is vital for African governments to systematically integrate environmental criteria into all aspects of economic decision making. Some 20 African countries have been working with the World Bank, which has only recently brushed up its own image, to formulate National Environmental Action Plans.

Lesotho, one of the first African countries to undertake such a programme, has been working to quantify the cost of soil erosion, in the hope that this will prompt policy makers to take concerted action against it. In response to the Koko toxic dumping episode, Nigeria has established a Federal Environmental Protection Agency, which recently issued guidelines on Environmental Pollution. Kenya has introduced environmental science as a compulsory subject in the national curriculum. Eight southern African countries have joined together to agree to a Zambezi River System Action Plan, to better manage the fragile resources of this river basin. All countries in the Southern African Development Co-ordination Conference (SADCC), are soon to subject major development projects to an Environmental Impact. Assessment (EIA).

The emergence of democracies

On the political front, undoubtedly the most notable development in Africa at the turn of the decade, and possibly the continent's biggest long term hope, has been the tide of pro-democracy movements sweeping through the continent. At the beginning of the decade, only six African countries — Botswana, Mauritius, Namibia, the Gambia, Zimbabwe and Senegal — claimed multiparty systems. Yet during the course of 1991, at least seven out of 53 African countries held multi-

party elections or reverted to political pluralism. Similar changes are in the works in close to two dozen African countries
at the time of writing. These changes have largely been
precipitated by worsening standards of living. As Zimbabwean
political scientist, and a respected African analyst, Jonathan
Moyo puts it, "You can't have economic problems, and fail to
blame those who are in charge."

Regional and international events have helped to strengthen
that conviction. Closest home, the release of Nelson Mandela
and mounting pressure for an eradication of South Africa's
oppressive apartheid system, have opened the eyes of many
to the political restrictions in their own countries. Mandela, for
example, faced one of the most embarrassing moments during
his African tours when the wives of two Kenyan politicians
detained for advocating political pluralism, urged the international celebrity to intercede on their behalf with President
Daniel Arap Moi. Closely associated with events in South Africa
has been the emergence of Namibia as Africa's youngest nation. Forged by seven diverse parties, the country's constitution
is one of the most democratic in Africa, and has become the
envy of many a citizen in neighbouring countries.

Nevertheless, democracy in Africa is still a fragile commodity.
In Kenya, for example, despite promised reforms, the Daniel
Arap Moi government in early 1992 brutally assaulted a group
of women protesters, including environmentalist Wangari
Maathai, who had gathered to demand the release of political
detainees. Leaders in Togo and Zaire, despite promising a
transition to pluralism, are still clinging to power, causing even
worse turmoil than before. Coups have been experienced in
Chad, Mali, and most recently in Sierra Leone. In Liberia and
Somalia, the overthrow of dictators left a vacuum that has led
to faction-fighting and near anarchy. But the end of the Cold
War, political changes in South Africa, and moves toward
democratisation are slowly leading to resolutions of some of
the continent's worst conflicts, most notably in Angola and
Ethiopia. This has given rise to optimism that military expenditure
in Africa, which accounts for $14 billion annually (roughly
equivalent to education spending, and four times the amount

spent on health) might gradually be diverted to positive pursuits.

Most important, the promise of democracy is giving Africa's people a new voice and energy. This spirit was captured when 500 delegates from women's groups, peasant movements, grassroots organisations, UN agencies and African and donor governments gathered in Arusha, Tanzania, under the auspices of the UN Economic Commission for Africa in 1990. In the African Charter for Popular Participation in Development and Transformation, participants called for immediate and far reaching changes so that people from all levels of society could join in the conception, planning and implementation of development strategies.

Specifically, the Charter called on governments to enhance access to land, credit and technology and expand literacy and training programmes; urged the equal status of women in social, political and economic spheres; and asked the international community to support indigenous efforts to foster democracy. "At no other time in the post-war period," says the Charter, "has popular participation had so astonishing and profound an impact; inevitably and irresistibly, popular participation will play a vital role in Africa."

Democracy and the environment

Democracy has been called the environment's best friend. The reason, as with almost any other issue, is that no matter what formal policies the government introduces, as long as the people who are affected by them are not part of the decision, or of the process of implementing or policing them, they will not succeed on the ground. As noted earlier, most governments now have in place policies, institutions and frameworks that address environmental issues directly, and in their broader context.

On their own, these are unlikely to amount to much. Africa abounds with examples of contour ridges, bunds and windbreaks, built under duress and, with no effort to involve the local community, that have simply been allowed to disintegrate. In Ethiopia, for instance, under the former socialist government of Mengistu Haile Mariam, peasant associations were obliged, in order to stop soil erosion, to construct thousands of kilometres of dry stone and earth walls called bunds. Millions of trees were also planted. Those who did not co-operate were fined. Today, there is precious little evidence of either the bunds or trees.

In Lesotho, notes a senior official, "Huge amounts of money have been spent on mechanical measures, like making terraces and waterways. But we have realised that there is one element missing. We have been ignoring the very people who are supposed to benefit from these measures." Now, he maintains, "There is a radical shift in thinking. We are concentrating on education, creating awareness, and popular participation. We are also looking at biological solutions, like afforestation, which have direct benefits for the farmer."

One such scheme has been to allow farmers to "own" dongas, provided they grow trees and demonstrate that they are arresting erosion. Because land is so short in Lesotho, farmers have been keen to take out shares in these dongas. Certificates, issued by the ministry of agriculture to successful applicants, add to the personal sense of responsibility; the trees planted in the dongas are useful to the farmers for roofing and fencing when they are fully grown. Farmers in the area have voluntarily organised themselves to build catchment dams at points along the slope to arrest the flow of water.

In an interview with the US-based *African Farmer* magazine, Robinson Gapare, President of the Zimbabwe National Farmers Association, which represents the views of small scale farmers, underlined the importance of consultation and co-operation between development agents, and those directly affected: "There is a tendency to say rural people are lazy, that they cannot think. As a peasant myself, I greatly resent that attitude. I personally think that rural people are some of the wisest people in the world. Let the rural people participate in the planning process. Ask them what their thinking is. Ask them how we can solve problems. Without this approach, no matter what your programme is, you will actually end up with a negative result."

In desperation, some governments have resorted to heavy-handed means. In Uganda, for example, President Yoweri Museveni has ordered an end to all indiscriminate tree-felling and has warned that he will invoke presidential powers to detain without trial those bent on destroying the country's forests. But many peasants — in Uganda and elsewhere in Africa — have no alternatives. New, improved cooking stoves that use less wood are one alternative being looked at, yet in many African countries these have failed to catch on. The reason is that unlike the open fire, the stoves do not give off heat and light, and interfere with the age-old custom of sitting around the fire at night. An appropriate technology expert in Harare tells of designing a fuel effective stove, which did not catch on because it was made out of garbage cans which offended the sensibilities of house-proud rural women. Socially acceptable alternatives, designed in consultation with the people concerned have, on the other hand, started to show promise.

Governments themselves often require policing and reminding of the environmental objectives they have set. In Botswana, regarded as one of the most democratic governments in Africa, the government has had to reluctantly back down on a controversial water development scheme, which involved dredging part of the Boro River in the ecologically fragile Okavanga swamp, to service the new diamond mining town of Maun. For seven hours, local residents and conservationists told the visiting Minister of Mineral and Water Resources, Archie Mogwe, that the scheme threatened their livelihoods as well as parts of the unique ecosystem. Their campaign was supported by local NGOs, as well as Greenpeace, the international environmental pressure group, which launched a "Diamonds are for Death" campaign against Botswana internationally.

In Zimbabwe, agitation by the Zambezi Society, a local non-governmental organisation, eventually forced the government to alter a contract with the huge multinational, Mobil Oil, which is prospecting for oil in the Zambezi Valley. With oil imports amounting to $75 million annually, Zimbabwe is understandably anxious to discover its own oil source. In its hurry, the government made no provision in the draft contract for an environmental impact assessment.

Working through the local press, the well respected Zambezi Society lost little time in pointing out that the country's National Conservation Strategy, launched a few years before, made EIAs compulsory for all development projects. As a result, the contract was revised, and the company is spending half a million dollars more to ensure that more environmentally sound exploration methods are employed.

In Zimbabwe, neighbouring Zambia and Botswana, several NGOs have been working with local people in innovative wildlife ranching schemes. The principle of these is that if poaching is to be stopped in the large game reserves, set aside for tourism, peasant farmers have to perceive some benefits from wildlife. Because, in the schemes, peasant farmers benefit from the revenues that accrue from wildlife — through legalised hunting, safaris, and from the by-products of the trade, like skin bags and ornaments — they are not tempted to poach.

Groups like the Communal Areas Management Programme for Indigenous Resources (Campfire) in Zimbabwe, are gradually altering western thinking on conservation, which has focussed on endangered species, as though they exist outside a socioeconomic environment. In many African countries, again, research is under way into traditional methods of intercropping, ploughing and use of natural manures and pesticides. These projects, which aim to reverse the negative effects of modern farming methods, involve tapping a reservoir of knowledge, particularly among older women, of fast dying traditions.

Local groups, determined to improve their immediate lot with or without government help, are mushrooming across the continent. The Zvichanka Farming Group in Zimbabwe, cited in the series of features presented here, is one example. In west Africa, the idea of one woman — Hawa Sawadogo of Burkina Faso — for women to come together and save enough money to buy a grinding mill has grown into a network of 3600 grassroots village development groups in six west African countries — Burkina Faso, Mali, Mauritania, Niger, Senegal and Togo. The movement is called "Six S", from its French name, which means "Using the Dry Season in the Savannah and the Sahel." It grants loans on easy terms to organised groups on the basis of clearly defined projects such as cereal banks, grain mills, improved livestock breeding, gardening crafts, vegetable drying, storing and weaving. Members of Six S, many of whom are women, are also engaged in the construction of barriers to hold back water seepage and fight bushfires; the construction of improved housing, and reforestation.

In Kenya, the Greenbelt Movement described in the profile of Wangari Maathai, has planted ten million trees. Maathai, one of the most articulate African environmentalists, has never hesitated to speak out against the broader framework in which environmental degradation occurs. Receiving the Africa Prize for Leadership for the Sustainable End of Hunger administered by the US-based Hunger Project in 1991 she asked, "And why are the hungry masses forced to repay loans that they never received, and debts that they never incurred ?" For Africa to avoid its own holocaust, she continued, the continent "requires brave, responsible, accountable leaders. It cannot afford the greed, the irresponsible leadership, the corruption, the plunder, the autocratic rule of fear and small wars."

Protesting in front of the Nairobi prison, against armed police and dogs, for the release of political prisoners, Maathai and her Greenbelt Movement have become a powerful symbol of how Kenyan women are fighting far more than just the immediate loss of their soil. Yet it is from that struggle that they have found their voice. As Maathai puts it, "Planting trees is something that can be done by people themselves. People in Africa have to know that you do not have to do big things. You can start at home by doing simple things, like planting trees."

Colleen Lowe Morna

KENYA

Rebuilding homes and communities
Rebecca Katumba

Nairobi — Women experts on housing gathered here in 1990 for an inter-regional seminar to explore methods of increasing the role of women in the management and development of settlements. The seminar was one of the activities of the Nairobi-based UN Centre for Human Settlements (Habitat) towards the implementation of the "Global Strategy for Shelter by the Year 2000" (GSS).

GSS is a Habitat initiative to assist governments in search of solutions to the problems of inadequate housing and sanitation. Some 30 "experts" attended the seminar. But the stars of the show were three Kenyan women who were attending an international conference for the first time in their lives. Unlike the rest, they were not highly educated. They had only worked with women's groups in their communities. But they had something that none of the other participants could claim: practical experience of inadequate shelter and poor sanitation.

In order to allow Zipporah Mweni, Nancy Wairimu Kimani and Rosalia Mutunga to make their presentation in Swahili, the UN rule on official languages had to be overlooked. Mweni is chairperson of a cooperative of 86 women's groups with 2,255 members in Kibwezi district in Kenya's eastern province. This district, northeast of Nairobi, suffered from the African drought of the early 1980s.

"Our men left Kibwezi to look for jobs. But many never returned, nor sent back money. After watching our children die we had to adjust to the fact that we were on our own and responsible for the children's future," Mweni told the participants. The hungry women then accepted the food-for-work programme introduced by the government and various non-governmental organizations.

The work focused on community projects. "Most of us saved on food and sold it and when exotic goats were brought in, we bought local goats for cross-breeding. Now we have goat's milk." The children of Kibwezi are the only ones in this east African country who depend on goat's milk. Cattle rearing is impossible due to the tsetse fly menace. "We keep bees and have managed to construct our own factory which refines our honey for both local and international markets," said Mweni. The community also farms fish and rears rabbits.

Until 1982, Kibwezi town which consisted of a road junction and an administrative building, was considered by the government as a hardship area. Today, it has a bank with the women as majority clients, hardware shop, health centre, restaurant and amenities like public telephone booths. "We have a school for our daughters, with the curriculum tailored to our needs, hoping that after finishing the girls will take over the activities of the community," Mweni told stunned participants. "Meanwhile, all the illiterate women are attending literacy classes."

The government encouraged women to build permanent dwellings. "The community has been revitalized and some of the men have started to come back. Wives have been counselled to accept them because the population has been unbalanced for some time," said Mweni.

Kimani and Mutunga belong to two women's cooperatives which own building materials factories. The factories were set up with help from African Housing Fund (AHF), established by Shelter Afrique in 1988 to assist African countries in providing housing for the poorest of the poor. AHF is Africa's response to the UN International Year of Shelter for the Homeless, an initiative which has not been duplicated in other regions.

Until Christmas eve 1988, Kimani was a squatter in Mathare valley, Nairobi's largest and oldest slum area. She was evicted with her family of eight and took refuge in a church. Together with 239 colleagues from four women's groups in Mathare, Kimani formed Humana, a cooperative society. They sought help from AHF, which trained them in building materials production and social and management skills. Humana has a factory which produces roofing tiles. Recently the women won a tender to supply tiles worth about US$ 250,000 to a middle income housing project in Nairobi. Most members who used to survive on bootlegging (brewing and selling a type of gin called changaa) now earn four times as much from factory work. Humana makes a monthly profit of about US$ 4,750. "We have acquired land in Dandora, a suburb of Nairobi and we are busy building houses for ourselves," Kimani announced proudly.

Mutanga is chairwoman of the Mungano Women's Group, a coalition of 33 groups in Kitui district also in the eastern province. It is a semi-arid area with farming as its mainstay. With an advance of US$ 400,000 from AHF, as part grant and part loan, members have been trained in the production of roofing tiles, blocks and cement slabs for improved toilets.

"We have a factory producing tiles and 20,000 litre tanks," said Mutanga. "It also employs 97 people, the majority of them women. It's the only one of its kind in the district. We have the largest group of employees with a regular income in Kabati which is a rural town."

The presentations of the three women stunned the gathering. Caroline Pezzulo, a consultant with Habitat, said, "What these women are doing cannot just be termed income generating activity. They are really building the community." Pezzulo said Habitat was interested in mobilizing women to fully participate in the effort to provide shelter.

"This is important because female-headed households are growing in number and are estimated at 43 per cent of the total number of families in sub-Saharan Africa," she said.

For women to be empowered, a myriad problems need to be solved. In sub-Saharan Africa, for instance, women are not allowed to inherit land. This reduces many of them to destitution on the death of their husbands. According to Pezullo, "whether urban or rural, women are the poorest of the poor." Safe shelter, sanitation, clean water and other facilities are their immediate concerns. Women are therefore committed advocates of the strategy to improve shelter. "Whoever is trying to help improve shelter should work through women's movements. That is the base," she concluded.

Greening takes root
Rebecca Katumba and *W. Akute*

Nairobi — When Wanjiri Wang'endo was a child, trees were taken for granted. Not so any more. Now trees are something the 68-year-old Wang'endo treasures. She dedicates much of her life to plants, nursing seedlings and nurturing trees in her neighbourhood. Once the small shoots sprout their first two leaves, she carefully uproots them and plants them in a field nearby. Wang'endo has already grown 70 trees from seedlings and says she will continue doing so until she dies.

Like thousands of other Kenyan women today, Wang'endo belongs to the Green Belt Movement, a community-based tree-planting campaign, which was started over a decade ago by a woman who could not bear to see the desertification of her nation. It was in 1977 that Kenya's first woman professor was moved enough to abandon her prestigious job as head of the department of anatomy at the University of Nairobi, and launch the campaign. Initiating a simple tree-planting drive, the spirited Wangari Maathai spurred her fellow-Kenyans to sit up and take note of the increasing barrenness around them.

"Since women use wood fuel for cooking and they also till the land, my focus was and still is on women,"says Maathai. "We work together to conserve what is remaining of our environment."

The movement is now one of the most successful women's

environmental projects in Kenya, with a membership of about 50,000 owning 1,500 tree nurseries. "We green belters are humble people," Maathai remarks. "Many have no money and are semi-literate but we have managed to come together and achieve our goals because of our commitment to the environment." Indeed, the group can boast of planting about seven million seedlings in 22 districts, and plans to cover the remaining 21 districts within the next five years. Although the Movement's headquarters is still a humble operation, it was involved over 600 women's groups, each of which has set up green belts with at least 1,000 trees. The women have also mobilised churches, schools and households in their efforts to halt deforestation.

Still, the task in Kenya, as elsewhere throughout the continent, is daunting. The quantity of firewood needed to satisfy Kenya's population of around 17 million far exceeds the supply. In 1985, the demand for firewood had reached 24.5 million tonnes against a supply of just 19.1 million tonnes. And official estimates project that by the year 2000 the demand will spiral to 47.1 million tonnes while the availability will dwindle to 16.5. "The impact of environmental degradation hits our women and children most," says Maathai. "They are the ones who remain in the villages struggling with it while the men flock to cities in search of jobs they may never find."

In this Movement which is primarily made up of women directly affected by the problem, experts are largely kept out of the programme because, as Maathai explains, "they have the tendency to work for the people rather than allow them to work for themselves." When organisations employ experts, she argues, "It does not encourage people to be masters of their own destiny. It disarms them, making them dependent, and at times apathetic." By contrast, the participatory approach makes women grow trees not just for the sake of trees, but because they want to.

The Green Belters plant and cultivate the seedlings, care for the trees and generate a source of income for themselves. Seedlings grown in nurseries are sold to the Movement and redistributed free to women for planting in fields on condition that they care for them under the supervision of a ranger.

The Movement pays for every tree that survives beyond the second month of replanting, and the price varies according to the type of tree. Women are advised to grow fruit trees to provide that extra bit of nourishment for their families. They are also encouraged to green any piece of land that they find lying idle — along roads, farm boundaries and market places.

But it has hardly been easy sailing for the Green Belt Movement and as Maathai can vouch, being an activist in Kenya has never been a simple task. Her struggles to protect the environment have, more often than not, landed her right in the middle of raging controversies. Towards the end of 1989, for instance, when she opposed the siting of the 60-80 storeyed *Kenya Times* complex in Uhuru Park, the only green belt left in the centre of Nairobi, she sparked off furious debate. But the battle was hardly unique, says Maathai, as environmentalists all over the world have similar confrontations with politicians. "But what I was not prepared for," she adds, "were the personal attacks, insults, ridicule and victimisation that were to follow."

Still, never one to give up, she took it as a lesson, thrilled that "the debate did not have any adverse effect on the Movement's activities. In fact, it boosted it and more people became environmentally conscious."

It also made Maathai keenly aware of the fact that leaders in the country need to be educated on environmental issues and that in Kenya, as elsewhere in the world, the government must integrate environment in its development plans. "Environment is yet to be taken with the seriousness it deserves. People must appreciate the linkages between environment, politics and the economy of a country," she says over and over again.

When Maathai was awarded an honorary doctorate of law by Williams College in Massachusetts, USA, for her role in environmental conservation, she saw it as yet another step towards a recognition of the environment.

Recognition for Maathai, meanwhile, has come from several other quarters as well. But what pleases Maathai as much as the international acclaim that has come her way, is the progress of the Green Belters in Kenya. The group soon hopes to construct its headquarters in Nairobi, with a training centre where people from all over the continent can be educated on environmental issues.

The Green Belt Movement has already received a number of requests from other African countries for training their people, but, as Maathai explains, "We cannot train people at the moment because we do not have a permanent base."

Still, the future looks bright and she is convinced that the women are on the right track, as most of the goals they set in 1977 have been achieved. "They recognise the need to have a good and sound environment which they can bequeath to their children," she says. And if that knowledge is ingrained indelibly, that's half the battle won. But what's more, if, like Wang'endo, Kenyan women no longer need to walk long distances for firewood, because they now have enough around them and even some to spare, that is an even surer sign of success.

Putting farmers on the agenda
Rebecca Katumba

Nairobi — Two years after her marriage, Maria Lubengo quit her job as a teacher and instead, gave all her attention to farming her 12-acre family plot. Today, the Luvusa farm, in the Moshi district of Tanzania's Kilimanjaro region, about 650 kms from capital Dar es Salaam, is among the few success stories of mixed farming in the area. But credit for this always goes to Lubengo's husband, Ian Luvusa, the owner of the plot.

As if this is not enough, Lubengo complains, whenever an extension worker wants to teach new skills or introduce new seeds, he always leaves word with her for her husband to attend. "So I've never been taught anything by an extension worker," explains Lubengo. "I just use the indigenous knowledge passed on to me by my parents and the little I learnt at school. Sometimes I follow the instructions my husband gives me when he has the time."

Recently, government officials left a message for her husband to expect visitors who were on a field trip after a workshop on 'Environment and the Poor' held in Arusha, about 80 kms from Moshi. "On the appointed date, my husband was here alright, but I was the one who answered almost all their questions because I am the one who works on the farm," recalls Lubengo.

It was precisely such problems that a recent workshop hoped to address. Held separately in two East African states — Kenya and Tanzania — the workshop on soil and water management for sustainable smallholder production, was attended by about 100 experts from 17 countries, mainly from eastern, central and southern Africa. It was organised by the World Association of Soil and Water Conservation, Southern Africa Development Coordination Conference, Swedish International Development Agency and the joint inter-disciplinary committees in Kenya and neighbouring Tanzania.

Discussions at the 13-day gathering were preceded by a meeting of sociologists and anthropologists in Kenyan capital Nairobi, where experts identified "insufficient attention paid to social issues by researchers, rather than lack of technical know-how," as the main stumbling-block to sustainable soil and water management. They observed that farmers' resisted past conservation measures probably because programmes were generally implemented without their active participation. Neither was there adequate analysis of the socio-economic constraints they face.

A report by Senegalese agronomist, Issa Beye, of the Environment Liaison Centre International in Nairobi, notes for instance, that there is a systematic bias against small-scale farmers, although they are the ones who produce most of the continent's food. "Such farmers are often regarded by the government as backward and resistant to change. They end up being isolated by the very people who are supposed to help them — research institutions, agronomists, bureaucrats and engineers," he points out.

And, according to the report, women farmers are even more neglected, despite the fact that they grow 80 per cent of Africa's food.

The recent workshop too identified what it called "the extension gap". The glaring neglect of thousands of African women farmers like Lubengo, by extension workers, most of whom are men, was seen as one of the major causes of declining crop yields and land degradation. Various reasons have been advanced for this. According to the World Bank Report, most of today's extension services grew out of the rural administrations of earlier colonial governments. Under these governments, extension activities normally focussed on the introduction of new crops for export. A Tanzanian sociologist, Charles Rwejuna, advanced another very real and immediate reason: that husbands resent their wives spending time with strangers (extension workers), "in other words, jealousy".

The participants agreed that one of the solutions lay in training more women to become extension workers. The Uyole Agriculture Centre, the largest training centre in Tanzania, has, for instance, only 133 women students out of the total of 474. In Zimbabwe, the workshop was told, out of a total of 2,000 extension workers, only 120 are women. Yet, despite recognition of past mistakes, the organisers of the workshop went ahead and excluded the participation of farmers, especially women, in this important meeting. And as Lubengo testified, even in their field trips to Arusha and Kilimanjaro where the women worked the land, a message was left for husbands to be in attendance.

Joseph Arap Leting, head of the Kenyan Public Service said that for too long, farmers have been considered an environmental problem rather than the solution, and lamented their exclusion in the decision-making process. The key to ending recurrent food shortages, concluded the workshop, was in reforming the entire system. This would include doing away with agricultural practices that deplete the soil, as well as policies which favour export crops instead of food crops.

But it would also mean controlling population growth and environmental degradation, and acknowledging the value of traditional farming knowledge, which hundreds of Africa's women farmers like Lubengo successfully apply to their own lands, when assistance from other quarters is not forthcoming.

Village women pack up and leave
Rebecca Katumba

Nairobi — More and more women who have lost their land are leaving their villages and streaming into Kenyan cities in search of work. While many of the migrant women are wives accompanying their husbands, "a large proportion are women who have lost their land or will not inherit because of discriminatory customs," according to UNICEF. "Their move to urban areas is, therefore, a permanent transfer."

Take Maria Mathai, for instance. Three weeks after her husband was buried, 28-year-old Mathai found that she and her four young daughters had no rights over the five-acre farm the family owned at Chaka, on the slopes of Mount Kenya, about 250 kms north-east of Nairobi. When the title deed arrived at the end of last year, it was in the name of her husband, John Mathai, a sound recordist with an audiovisual company, Visnews, who was killed in an explosion at an ammunition dump in neighbouring Ethiopia.

The widow has no son, and as in many African cultures, her Meru tradition does not entitle her to inherit, despite the fact that she worked the land more than her husband. Consequently, the chief of her husband's clan has asked her to move out of the village. But Mathai has nowhere to go, because her parents are not willing to have her back. She is, however, a little more fortunate than other women in her position. Her plight caught the attention of national media and funds are now being raised to buy her another farm. Other women in similar circumstances would either stay on in their villages to work as casual labourers or set off with their children to the city in search of a better life.

In an effort to stem the rising tide of migration from rural to urban areas, the Kenyan government is working on a land reform legislation that converts customary land tenure into freehold farms. The idea is that if farmers have security of tenure, production would automatically increase because farmers would then have the incentive to undertake permanent improvements, thus curbing resale of land which has left many women homeless.

But many feel the land tenure legislation has not helped women. "The legislation in actual fact suggests that access to land for women as a group is being systematically eroded," says Elizabeth Nzioki, who has researched into the effects of land tenure reform on women's access to and control of land for food production. Nzioki points out that land titles are being transferred almost exclusively to men, "thus transforming women's traditional access to land to that of simple labourers". And yet," she adds, "most of this land has been inherited and not bought by the men. In this country, women do not inherit land but all along, we have been depending on our husbands or in-laws to give us land to farm."

Since a woman can only have access to land that belongs to her husband, the increasing number of single mothers in rural areas are either forced to buy land if they can afford it or work as farm labourers. Nzioki says the legislation is of little use to women because they have almost no income. According to her, the only women who have benefitted from the new legislation are the affluent, and mostly with urban interests. In fact, she feels that the legislation has made for sharp rifts within society. "Rich farmers gain at the expense of poorer farmers, those with education and political power at the expense of those without, and men gain at the expense of women," she says.

The title deed is a valuable asset in rural Kenya, especially to get loans. But most women can never get a loan because they have no land titles. But worse still, the owner of a title deed has the right to mortgage his land without consulting the women who are actually cultivating it. While women still have access to land through their husbands and sons, Nzioki warns that the land tenure legislation has deprived them of the power to control the land they use. Women are being edged into marginalised land, thus further decreasing their productivity and making them even more marginal.

"This does not augur well with the government policy on

nutrition and food security where the strategy is to increase and diversify food production at the household level so that rural families are properly fed," Nzioki points out.

The land tenure reforms have also led to commercialisation of agriculture. But even as the income of farmers goes up with the growing of cash crops, the burdens on women increase. Women are now forced to work on farms controlled by their husbands at the expense of their own food crops and other income generating activities. And the money, of course, goes into the pockets of men, ensuring that women are deprived of control over the family income as well. The title deed, in short, has become a legal instrument empowering men to gain almost complete control over land and over women's labour.

A harvest of locusts
Bona Bringi

Nairobi — Ayuma Musoga, a caterer, remembers his childhood when a locust invasion was always welcome. Besides the excitement that went with the experience, the invasion always brought a promise of an endless supply of a tasty snack: fried locust.

The first time Musoga witnessed an invasion, she was only six.

Her mother would cut down the branch of a tree heavily laden with locusts and beat it against the ground. Before the dazed insects recovered from the shock, they were heaped into a hot frying pan where they would sizzle in their own fat. On cooling, the fried locusts would be stored in wide mesh baskets, to be eaten over a long period of time. "The locusts did not look very appealing, but they were tasty," recalls Musoga. "We children ate them at any time we chose and occasionally, they also served as the main protein dish."

Several African countries are still under siege as locusts, grasshoppers, armyworms, rats and birds threaten millions of acres of cropland and therefore, the survival of millions of people recovering from drought and famine, says a recent UN

Food and Agriculture Organisation (FAO) report.

Kenya, too, often faces locust invasions from neighbouring Tanzania, but Musoga suggests a way out. She feels that women should go back to using traditional methods of preserving locusts which would then serve as a cheap substitute for animal protein. "These methods may seem ineffective now, but by doing so, Kenyan women could help control the onslaught without using pesticides which pollute the environment," says she. Moreover, she points out, locust harvesting need not be confined to petty trade at village level. Instead, she anticipates a wider market where locusts could be introduced at tourist hotels as a local delicacy.

Musoga's proposal is not unique. Tanzania's agriculture and livestock minister, Paul Bomani, suggested recently that instead of relying entirely on pesticides, Africans start harvesting locusts and birds which are destroying tonnes of food in the continent. Bomani told a meeting of the Desert and Locust Control Organisation (DLCO) here that when spraying locusts, it was often forgotten that these pests were rich in protein. "Consequently, locusts, an excellent source of protein, just rot in Africa's jungles," he said.

The minister urged African countries to follow the example of China which had set up factories employing many people to process locusts for food. "If African governments harvested the pests, not only would the continent's hungry be fed, but it would also curb environmental pollution to a large extent," Bomani said. Harvesting locusts could also save Africa the exorbitant cost of controlling the scourge. According to FAO, US$ 50 million were spent in 1988 on locust control in Africa. At a meeting to evaluate the 1986 locust control campaign, held in Rome in December 1988, African experts put the cost of the operation at an estimated US$ 23.5 million.

FAO has also talked about the disturbing trend of proliferation among some migratory species of locusts, such as the desert locust, in countries bordering on the Red Sea. An extraordinarily large number of eggs are deposited in the soil in the Sahelian countries. Conservative estimates say the egg-infested area excluding the Sudan, spreads over 200 million hectares, extending from south-eastern Mali to the central-western region of Chad and passing through southern Niger and northern Nigeria. In southern and central Africa, the infestation covers 30 million hectares and includes parts of South Africa, Botswana, Zaire, Tanzania and Uganda.

With the current locust invasion showing no signs of an immediate let-up, it falls on African women who produce over 80 per cent of the continent's food crops, to come up with innovative ideas on food gathering, preservation and storage. This may well include harvesting locusts and other edible pests which threaten to reduce Africa to a continent of indigent people, ensnared by famine.

MALI

Toiling for total independence
Ramata Dia

Bamako — In the southernmost part of Mali, in west Africa, village women have got together to creatively use a 2,000 hectare ricefield. In village Niena, some 400 kms from Bamako, the Malian capital, women have traditionally helped their husbands with work in the fields. But they never received any kind of payment, and they had no right to own even a vegetable patch. But now with the help of a Malian company, Niena's women have thrown off their yoke and decided to become active participants in their region's development

After a small hydraulic dam came up in the area, these women worked hard at preparing their huge ricefield and today they take care of the production, management and marketing of the grain. In order to help them fulfill their new responsibilities, some of them were chosen by the government to undertake an eight-month training course in literacy, hygiene, agriculture and management techniques. When these women return to their village, they will train the other women and teach them what they were taught.

Just a month away from the rainy season, the women of Niena are getting their field ready. Equipped with agricultural tools, the ones who are trained measure the fields and estimate quantities of fertilizers, insecticides and weed-killers that will be needed. Others observe and get trained on the job. "Our objective is to gain perfect mastery of all the basic agricultural techniques," says Kiya Sidibe, a dynamic new farmer.

Accounts are maintained meticulously and the cash value of all borrowed inputs is calculated and paid up later. Each shareholder has an individual account and loans taken are noted down. "This way, we are sure not to find ourselves with inflated bills after the harvests," Sidibe explains, adding, "We make it a matter of principle to pay back the money that was lent to us to the last penny. We do not want to discourage those who trusted us."

The village men are unanimous in their admiration. "We have been surprised by their rigorous management and the output of their fields," they remark.

In their determination to become self-reliant, the women have collected savings, which, complemented by a small government loan, will help them set up a boring well, equipped with a manual pump. This will ensure healthy growth of seedlings before the first rains fall, and also augment the drinking water supply to the village. Taking advantage of this, the women will sell their harvest in the market before the other farmers, and at better prices. These earnings, as they say, will "help improve the menus at home, help with purchase of medicines and clothes for the family". This year, part of the profit has been used for the creation of a 10 ha. vegetable garden, producing tomatoes, cabbages, onions, lettuce and potatoes. Some of these are consumed locally, the rest are sold at weekly markets.

Despite the success of their enterprise, Niena's women still have several hurdles to cross, not least being the traditional prejudices against women's independence. For instance, most organisations giving agricultural loans prefer to give them to men. And when there is no money, they cannot get the proper tools. As the leader of the women farmers confides, "Till now we don't even have our own plough to work. We have to borrow it from the men. And sometimes they are so reluctant that we have to postpone the dates of ploughing." The women have therefore decided that the profits from the next harvest of the vegetable garden will be used to buy ploughs. Meantime, they do the work with their hands.

Another major problem is the lack of mills in the village and even 30 kms beyond. "It is tiresome to pound the grain, especially when we are pregnant," they explain. "We desperately need a grain mill, but it is very expensive." Assita, a 30-year-old mother of eight children who is six months pregnant again, voices another concern. "If only we could control the births, it would help us a lot."

Although Assita swears that this will be her last child, deep inside she is not at all sure. She wonders how she will manage, since the family planning team that was operating in the area, has left without notice. Niena's women think their departure was manoeuvered by the men to thwart their efforts towards total independence.

But they are not letting any of this get them down. As one of the gutsy village women says: "Even without ploughs and carts and with non-stop pregnancies, we shall not go back to where we were before."

MOROCCO

A water revolution
Bouchra Boulouiz

Marrakech — In a beautiful valley at the foot of the high Atlas mountains, life has remained unchanged for a thousand years, almost. The Berber tribals who live in the Dunein valley 150 kms from Morocco's capital, Marrakech, are a pastoral community who rear cattle and grow crops. Berber society is highly organised. Each village is ruled by the Jemaa, a council of adult males, which makes important decisions for the community, such as organising the division of labour and the distribution of water for irrigation and drinking.

Women divide their time between agricultural tasks, cattle rearing, gathering wood and fetching water and caring for their homes and children. Summers here are hot and dry and winters bring bitter cold and snow. Drought affects the valley periodically and finding potable water is a major problem for villagers.

"The nearest springs are two kilometres away from the hamlet. We have to get there early and return around midday," says a local woman, "so we can wash the children's clothes only once a month. Sometimes we have to carry up to 80 litres of water, and during the summer, we often go thirsty."

Water is also drawn from wells and taken to the hamlet where it is stored for days at a stretch, often in unhygienic conditions. The same water is used for drinking, washing and for animal troughs. Recently, UNICEF officials launched a project, Aqua I and II, to supply water to 54 hamlets in this remote valley. A multi-disciplinary team from the King Hassan II National Agricultural and Veterinary Institute is collaborating on the project.

Says Alami Mohammed of UNICEF, "This project addresses the chief concern of these communities : the distribution of water to each village. It involves the creation of a suitable infrastructure to distribute the water, and then educate people on the importance of sanitation, personal and collective hygiene, and the regular use of soap and water." The notion of hygiene here is "unscientific and is linked to religious belief," says Mohammed. "Still water is considered contaminated and moving water is assumed to be pure. The concept of bacteria is unknown to these people. They don't understand that fecal matter carries infections. "

A quarter of all children in this area die before their fifth birthday, "and that is an enormous proportion," says Mohammed. None of the houses here have toilets. In fact, the concept of toilets is alien to Moroccan culture. Only eight per cent of all homes in the country have toilets. People normaly use distant fields, far away from prying eyes. Defecation is not permitted in the village, except by small children.

The introduction of community toilets has created a revolution in the habits of these rural people. The toilets have been built with strict adherence to the Muslim custom of separating women from men. Traditionally, men bathe at the mosque, this being a place of worship and purification, associated with holy ablutions. Women and children bathe in small cubicles built of red laurel wood, which they build themselves.

But in five hamlets these habits are beginning to change. Here sanitary complexes have been built, consisting of a mosque, a hamam (public bath), a laundry, toilets and water troughs for livestock. In addition, an improved 'Koranic' classroom has been built. Traditionally, all teaching is done through the Koranic school where the holy book is memorised. Now a hygiene education project is being introduced for children.

What is most heartening is the level of community participation. "The originality of this project lies in the direct participation of the villagers in the process of decision-making, planning the work, and the use of their own financial and human resources," explains Mohammed. In fact, 60 per cent of the funds are provided by the local people with UNICEF contributing the rest.

"The villagers organise and carry out the work according to a time-table which governs their daily agricultural chores," says Tamim Mohamed, the group's economist and coordinator. "Labour is freely supplied by each community, taking into account its own organisation, the number of families, the amount of water needed, and the collective deployment of workers from each hamlet."

Slowly but surely, change is coming to the Dunein valley.

MOZAMBIQUE

Not quite out of the woods
Rachel Waterhouse

Nampula — The wooded landscape of Nampula province in northern Mozambique, with its shrubs and mahoganies, teaks and evergreens, once offered shelter and resources to Nampulan women. The harmony is now broken. Guerilla warfare, raging for over 10 years in the countryside, forced a sudden divorce between peasant-farmer women and the forests. Urban areas are swollen with refugees and the forest has been emptied of people. Under heavy pressure from the increasing population, the woodland is rapidly receding like a shrinking hairline around balding cities.

And the worst affected by deforestation are women.

But the government, non-governmental organisations and women at local levels who are anxiously rethinking ways of protecting what is left of their woodlands, may be just in time to stop an ecological disaster.

Women are the majority (52 per cent) in this coastal, southern African country's estimated 15 million people, and according to government figures, 97 per cent of them work in agriculture, mainly as subsistence farmers. Like elsewhere in the continent, they too grow food for the family, fetch firewood and water, and care for the family's health and home. In Nampula, all these tasks are growing harder by the day due to increasing deforestation.

"I leave home at 4.00 a.m. to walk to my field and get there just before 7.00. I work till nearly noon, when the sun gets too hot. Then I walk home again, but I get so tired, I go only every other day," laments Aacha Momade. She belongs to an informal association of more than 80 women, formed by women cooperative farmers working the green zone areas around Nampula town, the provincial capital.

Once, Momade's field was much nearer home. "But then the war and confusion came," she explains, and refugees flooded the city, swelling its numbers from 125,000 people in 1980 to almost 500,000 by 1991. Now there is stiff competition for land and firewood in a country where almost all cooking is done over an open woodfire. Only a tiny urban elite have the luxury of gas or electricity.

"I used to get firewood on my field, but there's barely enough wood to burn for fertiliser anymore," Momade says. "And although it's expensive, I have to buy from traders. I'd have to go 20 kms on foot to fetch it myself, and a woman with a baby on her back and other work, can't manage."

Last year, the worst problem for her group was soil erosion. Suhura Assane, of the same cooperative, says the early rains washed away seeds and young plants as the fertile top-soil was swept off their hillside fields, down rain-etched gulleys. "In normal circumstances, people wouldn't even try to farm this poor, sandy soil near town. But then further out, it's too dangerous now because of war," Wayne Teale, American forest expert, points out.

Since war refugees flooded in, demand for land and firewood is forcing people to cut trees and dig their fields ever higher up the hillsides around town. Vital tree cover is lost, and so are the roots which used to fertilise the soil and hold it in place when the rains came. Not only is erosion harming the fields, but it is threatening the very homes women live in, close to the town, for safety.

In the poor suburbs of Nampula, with no paved roadways, each small house of mud, wood and plaster has become an island, perched on a hillock of land, facing its neighbours across deep caverns cut out by the rain water." Last year, part of my house just washed away," recalls another member of the women's group, Tijola Mucusette. "I'm trying to reinforce it now, as there's nowhere else to build." Agriculturalists in Nampula explain that evergreens on the hilltops once used to catch the heavy rain and let it drip slowly onto the earth where it collected and then ran gently underground into streams, and eventually, rivers. Deforestation means there's nothing left now to break the rainfall. Come the downpour, water gushes down the hillside carrying away the soil and silting up rivers as well as the city's water reserve. Nothing is left to feed the rivers in the dry season. Soon, they could run empty for half the year.

A decade ago, foreseeing the risk of deforestation as the urban population grew, the government planned a forestry programme which aimed to supply Nampula town with 60 per cent of its fuelwood needs. But little has been achieved. Assistant director of the forestry project, S.Miguel, says the early scheme to plant 750 hectares of new forest every year for 10 years, was too ambitious by far, even without the effects of war. Teale, who assists the programme, says this year even the revised target of planting 300 hectares will not be met. And currently, the total plantation area of 1,700 hectares can only furnish 10 per cent of the city's fuel needs. Regular firewood sales are only planned to begin in 1995.

Regina Cruz of the provincial forestry department feels that isolated tree plantations which will never fully meet the need for fuel, is not the best use of land. Way below target, the project is already short of land to plant on. Long term solutions must take new circumstances into account. When war eventually ends, some people will leave the urban areas for the vast woodland which is still out there, beckoning but deadly.

Still, the permanent urban and peri-urban population of Nampula has grown. And to meet its need for trees, for fertile soil in a fixed place and for preventing soil erosion, Cruz's department began a forestry extension programme this year, designed to promote agro-forestry. "The main idea of the programme is that people can benefit from growing their own trees instead of relying on wild wood. They could grow their own fuel, protect the soil, fertilise it with leaves and so increase their farm production and income," she explains. Other benefits foreseen include improving the family diet by choosing to grow fruit trees.

To launch the idea, the forestry department plans to give out 5000 eucalyptus, cashew as well as citrus fruit seedlings this season to farmers, to plant as hedges around their fields. Cruz admits it will take time for the scheme to catch on. Trees grow slowly and it is a long while before the results are evident — leaving many a farmer reluctant to even try.

The women's group, meanwhile, is busy with its own alternatives. Last year, some of the cooperative farms the women belong to began contour ploughing and planting hedgerows of sisal or elephant grass to prevent soil erosion. Teale showed the women how to dig ridges along the contours of the land, to hold the rain water and stop their seeds getting washed away again. This season, the women say, they hope to cover the whole hillside with ridges.

"It's hard labour, but the method is working. It's keeping our crops in place, our fields are looking beautiful and other people come to see, then go away and copy what we do," says Assane proudly.

Now that trees are in short supply, the practice of mixing other organic matter with the soil to make it fertile, is also catching on. Another idea the women are exploring is to look for alternative stoves which can help save on fuelwood for cooking. Cruz warns that without such measures to halt deforestation, rivers will run dry, silts get poorer and erosion worse. Consequently, women farmers will find it ever harder to survive as they trek out farther still, in search of fuelwood and somewhere fertile to dig their fields.

But from little acorns do big oak trees grow. Women in the field and in the forestry department are busy working on a range of options. They may yet hold their land in place, and have trees growing again in Nampula before the heavy rains erode their livelihood.

Irrigation scheme leaves farmers high and dry
Rachel Waterhouse

Sabie — When the dam over the Sabie river was almost complete, thousands of women farmers thought their problems were nearly over. They had often been told that the multimillion dollar dam in the Mozambique's southern region would protect them from drought and floods, that it would help them grow as prosperous as their absent husbands — migrant workers in neighbouring South Africa.

But, in fact, their troubles have only just begun. The Sabie project has run out of funds, and plans for irrigation, accompanied by a brand new social services infrastructure, have been nearly jettisoned. The original concept of an integrated development project drawn up in 1981, was meant to bring water and social services to local people. Small farmers in particular, would benefit. But the Mozambique government has since revised its policy. It is now advertising vigorously to attract largescale private and foreign agribusiness to Sabie. This thrust not only excludes Sabie women from the benefits of the dam but may even push them out of their homes to haunt the margins of expensive, irrigated land.

Agriculture has always posed problems for Sabie women, who comprise the majority of small-scale and subsistence farmers in this area of southern Maputo province. Two rivers, the Nkomati and its Sabie tributary, should ensure a rich water supply to the region. However, vagaries of the weather — floods one year followed by drought the next — cause the rivers to either flood or dry to a trickle. The Corumana dam, built at a cost of US$ 169 million, was meant to end all that by controlling floods, holding back the river in a 103 sq km reservoir, and releasing water downstream to irrigate a planned 30,000 hectares of land.

Italy provided grants and soft loans to start construction of the dam in 1985, using Italian equipment and technical staff. Last year when the dam was nearly complete, the authorities switched their attention to irrigation channels in Sabie. "Sabie water is now stuck at Corumana," explains national director for water affairs, Policarp Napica. "While Italian funding for the dam itself has ended, the two main gates and central irrigation channel are missing."

Most of the money that sponsors promised for irrigation has either failed to materialise or has been withdrawn. East Germany, one of the earlier sponsors, no longer exists and the erstwhile Soviet Union has gone back on a substantial commitment. Other investors have been kept away by the changing international political climate and poor secutiry in Mozambique, after 15 years of civil war waged by the South Africa-backed 'Renamo' rebels.

Like most other regions here, Sabie too has not escaped the ravages of war. Since the mid-1980s, Renamo attacks have ruined agriculture here leaving most of the countryside empty as farmers fled rebel onslaught. In its attempts to restore peace and revitalise the war-ruined national economy, government policy in Mozambique has swung from socialism and state planning to a liberal, free market economy. Ties with old socialist allies in the east have crumbled and government is looking to the west for more credit, while encouraging private and foreign investment to fill the gaping hole in finance for development.

The Sabie project is caught in the middle of this rapidly changing scenario. Instead of 30,000 hectares only 2,000 hectares of land are actually being developed, under the supervision of the ministry of agriculture, with Italian funding. Currently, the only land fed by the new irrigation channels is a 100 hectare 'experimental field'. Some Sabie women complain bitterly that instead of receiving adequate benefit from the project, they have been moved to make way for the experimental field and an airstrip.

The first time Sabie's farmers became aware of the 'development' plans was in 1986, when dam construction at Corumana stopped their water supply and the local farmers' association had to struggle to get it back. Ironically, the advent of this 'development' has been such that Sabie is still characterised by drought.

Atalia Sithole grows maize and sweet potatoes on her one hectare plot. She is glad the flooding has ended. But this year has brought a new problem: her crop was burnt out by hot sun and lack of water. "I spend every day working on the land, from early morning till late. Maybe that's why nobody told me about the irrigation and how I can get it to my field," says Sithole.

There is no sign of the new schools and hospitals outlined

fund provided is inadequate to equip even the small health centre that thousands of Sabie women depend on, or to build classrooms for the school. According to the locals, the main advantage of the project so far, is improved security in the town of Sabie, where over a third of the people are displaced villagers who fled rebel attacks in the surrounding countryside. Since 1991, 800 soldiers have been stationed here.

Cooperative farmer Cacilda Mioche points out another 'advantage': "When local maize died of drought this year, at least I could buy maize from the project field, watered by expensive pumps and hosepipes far beyond the price range of my co-op." The next 500 ha. of land to be irrigated is earmarked for use by local small-scale and subsistence farmers. Initially, the water tax is likely to be low. But "once irrigation is completed in Sabie, farmers will have to pay for the service," points out the Italian project coordinator, Bruno Musti. "And after three to five years, peasant farmers either have to make a profit or risk being moved out."

To cover irrigation costs and make profitable use of the land, most of the Sabie area is now set for lease to foreign and private investors, while small plots could be auctioned for leasehold. Investment proposals already received by the ministry of agriculture include a 15,000 ha. mango plantation to be run by a Luxembourg based enterprise and a 6,000 ha. cattle ranch to be managed by South Africans. Musti expects that "over 50 per cent of local farmers will fail to make it." And Mozambican project coordinator Abel Jaime admits that "competition will be tough for local women. It could be hard persuading them to leave their land and make way for new irrigation channels."

The majority of women subsistence farmers could end up with no irrigation and perhaps even no land — worse off than before "development" started in their region.

This, then, is the irony of Sabie.

NAMIBIA

Neglected farmers hope for a new deal
Colleen Lowe Morna

Ondangwa — For years, Elizabeth Petros, a farmer who lives near this tiny northern Namibian town, has stoically tilled the hard soil of this semi-arid region. Like many other men here, Petros' husband works in Ondangwa, as a caretaker at a government office. But that, says Petros, "brings in only enough money to pay for the children's school fees and medical bills. It is not enough to feed four or five children." As a result, she farms a four acre plot, 15 kms outside the town, where she grows mainly mahunga, or millet, a drought resistant crop.

During South Africa's occupation of Namibia, which ended when the country became independent on March 21 1990, Petros received no government assistance in her efforts. "I have never been visited by any extension worker, I have never received any credit, I have never used fertilisers, and I have never produced any crops for sale," she says. But since independence, the government has declared its intention to support small-scale farmers, and Petros is hopeful :"We are expecting many things to change for us farmers."

Under South African rule, Namibia was carved up into 11 ethnic 'homelands,' which occupied a mere 25 per cent of this vast, semi-arid southwest African country. Some 15 per cent of the country was designated as nature reserves, and as much as 65 per cent reserved for the country's six per cent white population. The latter was later opened to all commercial farmers but very few blacks had the money to buy land in this zone.

Although agriculture accounts for only six per cent of Namibia's GNP, 70 per cent of the population is directly or indirectly dependent on farming for a living. Because of the

long tradition of men like Petros' husband, of going to the
towns, mines or commercial farms to look for work, most of
the country's farmers are women. Agriculture has been
neglected in Namibia primarily because of South Africa's
policy of selling its surplus cheaply in this country. But this is
far more pronounced in the black-dominated small-scale
sector, which South African authorities cared little about, than
in the white-dominated commercial sector, where farmers are
heavily subsidised.

A recent UN study of the northern Owamboland province,
where about half of Namibia's people live, found no agricultural extension work being done because the diplomas being
offered by the local training college were not recognised in the
rest of the country. In the circumstances, the report comments,
it is hardly surprising that no one wanted to train as an extension worker. Similarly, in the past, authorities set up several
demonstration farms, purportedly to teach better agricultural
methods. But, according to farmers, these simply produced
exotic fruit and vegetables for the South African Defence
Forces who had bases in the north before independence.

Although the Forces have now left and the war has ended,
the South West Africa People's Organisation (SWAPO), led by
Sam Nujoma, has some tricky policy issues to deal with. Unlike
Zimbabwe, there is no fund in Namibia to buy back land from
whites for resettlement of peasant farmers. The government,
which is trying to attract foreign investors, has pledged that it
will not expropriate any land. Namibia is also keen to reduce
its food dependence on South Africa, and sees large-scale
commercial farming, particularly in the well-watered Caprivi
strip, as the quickest way of doing this.

But in a keynote address made soon after independence,
Nujoma conceded that for a long time to come, the majority
of Namibians will have to make a living from small-scale
farming. Taking an example from Zimbabwe, where peasant
farmers have increased their market output tenfold since
independence in 1980, Nujoma stresses that the government
"stands ready to help small-scale farmers by a variety of
means".

The UN report on Owamboland estimates that with a minimum of better inputs and support services, the crop in this province could be increased by 200 per cent in two seasons, and by upto 400 per cent thereafter.

"What we need most is new ideas," said Petros, as she stood in the shade of a thorn-tree outside her neat row of huts, discussing the sort of measures which would make a difference to her life . "We need people to come and advise us about our soil. What we should do to make it more fertile, and the kind of crops we can grow. "We also need access to credit. If I could get a loan, I would put a pipeline to the nearest water supply, for a steady supply of water to my plot. This would help me in the drought years that we frequently experience here." Water would also enable her to grow two crops a year, so that she does not waste time during the dry season. "I think our government must seriously look into the issue of water,"she says. Like many other women, Petros would also be grateful for any technology which would ease her workload. "I plough all these fields myself with this short hoe. Even if I had a few oxen to help me plough, it would make a big difference," she says. When told about the successes of small-scale farmers, especially women, in neighbouring Zimbabwe, the Namibian farmer's face lights up. "I would like to visit this country. It should not only be the educated people who go on such trips. We farmers would also like a chance to see what is happening in other countries," says Petros.

SUDAN

Small enterprise, big success
Neimat M. Bilal

Khartoum — Severe drought and desertification over recent years has driven the traditionally rural Sudanese into cities in search of work. These displaced farmers, many of whom are women, find themselves forced into unfamiliar occupations in

the nation's informal sector. According to a Sudanese economist, about 70 per cent of business people in this country
are in the informal economy or engaged in informal trade with
neighbouring countries. And as the rural-urban migration continues unabated, increasing numbers of women find a niche
for themselves in the marketplace.

As they set about organising their activities, it is difficult to
believe that not so long ago, these women were more adept
at cultivating cotton, millet or sesame than at selling pins,
combs and sweets on Khartoum's bustling streets. Most of
them work out a system of sharing transport in the early hours
of the morning to bring their goods to the market.

"They are very systematic and punctual," explains a taxi-
driver who ferries groups of women to the market each day.
"And with so many of them sharing the cab, I make a greater
profit with them than I do on normal passengers."

The women usually lack the initial capital to start their
informal business. However, with inimitable initiative, they
manage to obtain money from various sources. "We get our
money, as loans, either from relatives or from merchants to
whom we have to pay interest, often as high as 50 per cent,"
says Halima, a trader in Khartoum's Omdurman market. Often,
merchants too loan fairly substantial sums of money to women
who have proved themselves trustworthy. For instance, Halima
was loaned a capital of Sudanese pounds (SL) 2000 (about US$
400) by a trader when she wanted to establish her business; she
repaid this money along with an interest of SL 1000 (about US$
200) within seven months.

Today, Halima's is a success story in Sudan's informal sector.
Apart from some cafes, she also owns several shops in Omdurman selling kissra, the traditional Sudanese bread.

But most informal businesses operated by women tend to be
small and home-based. These generally involve dress-making
and cooking. In Khartoum, for example, many women run
illegal clothes shops or small restaurants either in their own
houses or in the neighbourhood. Perhaps because they do not
possess a licence, many of them prefer working out of their
homes rather than from public places. It is a more passive

method of selling, where they wait for their customers to come
to them. Inevitably, such a system lapses into non-productivity,
and because of the informality of the methods, many women
find that relatives and friends take advantage of them — by
ordering items they never pay for or expect discounts on.

While many rural migrants to Khartoum establish their own
business, some are employed by others to market goods and
share in the profits. One merchant says that he employs young
women to sell women's clothes to those residents who cannot
venture into Khartoum to shop. "Rural women are hardwor-
king, sincere and patient," he says. "And they do good work
with you until, of course, they get married or gain enough
experience to launch their own business."

Most of the women who work in the informal sector are
illiterate and this becomes a major obstacle, limiting their
opportunities. For instance, they cannot approach lending
institutions or initiate procedures to formalise their activities.
It was precisely to help them in this area that 'Estern Stete' was
established in 1984 by Euro Action Accord, a non-governmental organisation in Port Sudan. This programme provides loans
and training facilities to small producers.

"Rural migrants, refugees, the aged, the disabled, all come
under the purview of our programme," explains Ali Adam, the
coordinator. "We give them the necessary support to develop
their skills and their business and through this we try to incul-
cate the concept of self-reliance."

However, there are certain conditions to be met before the
programme can lend support. These conditions are that the
person has a family to support, that he or she has a business
with potential to be developed and that the person has been
living in the area for not less than two years. The entrepreneurs
are given a two-month grace period after which they start
repaying their loans from their profits. And according to the
consultants, "none of the women clients have failed to repay
the loans. In fact, a great number of them repay even before
their deadline." Women who do have problems with payments
are encouraged to discuss them with the consultants, who then
visit them regularly to try and identify the problems and work

towards removing them. If the difficulties are with the business itself, the women are either given more training or are encouraged to shift to a new, more conducive venture. If the problems are domestic, the women are given a further grace period.

Since the programme started six years ago, 1,984 women have been assisted in their business, out of a total of 4,341 clients. One of the contributing factors to the success of the programme is the close relationship which the consultants build with the women, and therefore their familiarity with every aspect of the business they fund. "Although many of the women still complain about little things like the scarcity of one or another raw material or its high price, you cannot help but notice the tone of great pride as they talk of their business," notes Nafisa Raheim, a journalist.

And in the words of one of the beneficiaries, "We realise that our business is very small, but we see the positive changes in our families and also in ourselves as women."

TUNISIA

Gobbling up the forests
Essma Ben Hamida

Tunis — In the mountainous areas of northwest Tunisia, women spend three to four hours a day collecting firewood. Every year each family burns four and a half tons of wood just to bake bread.

It hardly comes as a surprise, therefore, that Tunisia's forest cover has been declining at an alarming pace. An estimated three million hectares of forests covered Tunisia during the Roman era, 2000 years ago. By the end of the 19th century, that figure had more than halved and by 1956 — the year of Tunisia's independence from France — less than 400,000 ha. remained.

In the northwestern Kef region, once renowned for its magnificent aleppo pines and cork oaks, forested areas declined by 40 per cent between 1950 and 1986. Even areas qualified as wooded are often sparsely covered. The shrinking of the forest cover accelerated soil erosion, modified the climate and dried up underground water sources, seriously affecting the country's agriculture. Such acute deforestation has several causes: commercial exploitation which reforestation has not been able to compensated (only 260,000 ha. have been planted in Tunisia since 1956), and overgrazing of livestock in forest areas. However, unauthorised firewood collection too is to be blamed for the environmental degradation.

About 90 percent of the region's 29,000 rural families use firewood and on average burn 4.5 tons of wood every year. A study undertaken in Kef in early 1990 by the German Technical Cooperation Agency (GTZ) and the national energy agency, estimated that in 1989 the country needed 123,000 tonnes of firewood but faced a deficit of 80,000 tons. With the population explosion in the rural areas, available dead wood has become insufficient. Increasingly, young trees are being chopped down, reducing future wood availability.

But sociologist Khalil Zamiti points out that, paradoxically, despite deforestation, forest resources are grossly under-exploited. This apparent contradiction is explained by the fact that mature tree trunks are too large and unwieldy to be chopped up and often rot away while young growth is destroyed. "Because of their fear of the foresters, women stealthily kill young trees by gradually chopping at the trunk with sharpened horse-shoes. This allows them to abide by the law and gather only dead wood," says Zamiti.

Gathering wood is time-consuming for the women. The weights they carry can be considerable. Each load typically weighs 30 kgs but can also sometimes be as much as 70 kgs — a lot for an undernourished woman. Carrying such heavy loads on the head or back often leave the women with serious health problems.

Wood is used for heating and cooking throughout Kef. But no less than 80 per cent of all wood consumed is used simply to bake bread in the traditional tabouna (clay oven). The tabouna is filled with wood which is fired to heat the oven, an operation which takes an hour. Then, flat cakes of dough are stuck to the pre-heated sides of the oven to bake. The women who collect the wood and do the baking are thus doubly exposed to health risks. Cooking over woodfires is a long process, often lasting several hours, during which they breathe in great quantities of smoke. In summer the cooking takes place outdoors. In winter, woodfires are burned inside the single-room dwelling. Often there is no chimney and the whole family is affected by the smoke.

The Kef study found that the energy efficiency of commonly-used wood burning appliances is poor. The tabouna uses only 10 per cent of the wood's energy, with the rest going up in smoke. And the inefficiency of the three-stone fireplace (on which most of the cooking is done) is only too well-known.

The study has come up with several suggestions for reducing wood consumption and diminishing health problems related to cooking. The proposals include a collective oven for baking bread which should reduce wood consumption by almost half, a better-designed hearth with a chimney, and an iron griddle for cooking, to replace the clay griddle. But the study stresses that improving the use of firewood is just a partial solution. Even if the proposed measures were introduced rapidly, a fuelwood deficit would remain, though it would be only 48,000 tonnes by 2001. To achieve real improvements, forest destruction must cease and forest regeneration be stepped up.

More rational exploitation of existing forest resources should put an end to destructive practices like overgrazing. When an animal nibbles at the bud of a young pine tree, no less than ten metres of potential growth is sacrificed: instead of reaching the normal 18 metres, the tree will probably grow to only eight. The study also recommends associating forest dwellers, after training, with forestry operations such as clearing undergrowth and pruning. The people could keep the branches thus cut for their own use. Perhaps more important, forestry staff should come to be seen as allies in the effort to protect the forest, rather than as

Oppressors stopping people from gathering essential fuel.

As for regeneration, it recommends a vigorous replanting programme, including the use of fast growing species. But unless forest dwellers, and particularly women, are fully associated with this programme, it is unlikely to be successful.

Still, the study expects these measures and the new forestry code adopted by the Tunisian government to lead to considerable improvements. But not before voicing a word of warning, that if appropriate measures are not taken, Tunisia's fuelwood deficit "will reach disastrous proportions" by the end of the century.

UGANDA

A home-building factory
Rebecca Katumba

Masese — Once landless, semi-literate, unskilled and unemployed, today the women of Masese are proud factory owners. "We are the only women in this east African country to own a building materials factory," says Lovinsa Tibita, 48, a divorcee and treasurer of the Masese Women's Cooperative at Jinja, about 80 kms east of the capital, Kampala.

Masese, with a population of about 10,000 is a slum area of Jinja, Uganda's second largest and erstwhile major industrial town. Due to civil strife and resultant economic problems in the country, many factories were forced to close, rendering hundreds of Ugandans jobless. Those employed get very low salaries, with the better-paid employee earning a meagre Uganda Shillings (US) 6,000 (US$ 25) a month.

Recent years have seen massive migration, especially of men, to other countries including Kenya, and very few of them keep their promises of sending for the rest of the family later, let alone sending money back home. The number of single parents, thus, is high and prostitution rife.

"Rent for a one-roomed thatched house made of mud and wattle starts from US 700 (US$ 2) to US 2,500 (US$ 7). But even this is very expensive. So most of us supplement our income by brewing and selling traditional beer and waragi (a crude form of gin)," Tibita explains. Betty Akela, 28, a single parent and chairwoman of the 700-member cooperative, adds: "It's very difficult to find a job, especially if you are semi-literate and a woman." (The literacy rate among Uganda's 14 million people is 50 per cent for men and 29 per cent for women.)

"Apart from finding employment, our other problem has been housing. Many of us were born here," says Akela. "There's no other place we can call home except Masese. But we have been at the mercy of the Jinja municipal council." Anne Magezi, legal adviser to the cooperative explains that these women were squatters on council land and were threatened with eviction annually. "Some have been squatters from as far back as 1964. But they can only get a one-year lease, renewable annually at the discretion of the council," she adds. These people were tenants on sufferance. The council could evict them at short notice. Moreover, they were not allowed to build permanent houses or plant cash crops.

"Realising our predicament, we formed a self-help group," says Akela. "We started by rearing local chickens which we sold to buy 150 high-breed layers. We now sell eggs and we also make baskets, mats and table-cloths for sale."

It was around this time that the African Housing Fund (AHF) thought of setting up a pilot project in Uganda. Ingrid Munro, programme manager at AHF, explains: "We found that the Masese women met our criteria, especially as they were organised to better the well-being of their families." Uganda is one of the founder members of the AHF established in 1988. The Fund aims at improving the living conditions and financial status of the poorest of the poor among African women in both urban and rural areas. Uganda, along with Kenya, Burundi, Guinea and Zambia were chosen to provide models for pilot projects. Three projects have already taken off in neighbouring Kenya.

The Masese cooperative, according to Munro, has been given about US 395 million (US$ 100,000) as part grant and part loan by AHF. Moreover, the municipal council has allocated

10 hectares of land to them, to be extended as the need arises. The project was started in early 1990 and already the women have completed the factory and office buildings. They produce roofing and floor tiles, construction blocks and water tanks.

"We started with these as a training exercise to improve the quality of materials," Akela recalls. But soon now, the women will begin constructing houses for the cooperative members, and they hope that within two years every member will own a two-bedroom house, a 20,000-litre water tank and a ventilated pit latrine. They also have plans to build playgrounds and a daycare centre so that the children are well looked after. The factory directly employs 106 women at a salary of US 17,000 (US$ 45) a month. It also sells small quantities of building materials in the open market to enable women to make some money to repay the loan. Sadly, the men of Masese are unhappy about the project which has reversed their role as providers and owners of homes. They started off being skeptical of the women's ability to work in the factory. Now, because of job shortages, they are lobbying for employment for themselves in the factory. They also want the houses to be registered in their names instead of their wives'.

But as Akela says, "We are not giving in. We want to participate actively in post-war reconstruction. The men will soon see sense, especially when they realise that the children are now better fed, better educated and have a better roof over their heads."

AIDS orphans one million
Rebecca Katumba

Kampala — In a banana shamba (grove), behind a dilapidated mud-and-wattle hut, about 20 children between four and nine years old play a strange game of make-believe. It's a game they call 'Funeral,' in which they use heaps of stones to mark rows of graves.

But if visitors are taken aback by this funereal pastime, it does not surprise 65-year-old widow, Esteli Namubiru, as she watches them. "For the last two years or so," she explains, "we have had no weddings in this neighbourhood. Just funerals." In that period, Namubiru lost three sons and two daughters-in-law to AIDS. A third daughter-in-law looks deceptively healthy, but Namubiru knows that sooner or later, she too will succumb to the disease.

Today, in her village of Kasensero, in Rakai district about 180 kms southwest of the Ugandan capital, Kampala, Namubiru spends most of her time looking after 18 children orphaned by AIDS. Their ages vary between a year-and-a-half to 15. A few houses away, 70-year-old Haji Ibrahim Busungu sits on the verandah with a distant look in his eyes. He points to the mounds of red soil behind the house. "Those are the graves of my loved ones," he sighs. Busungu looks after nine orphaned grandchildren.

Under normal circumstances, these grandchildren would have brought sunshine into the lives of the old folk. But today, they have become grim reminders of death which has snatched away scores of young people. And the shadow hovers sinisterly over the children playing in the sun. For nobody knows yet if these orphans are AIDS-affected, too. Like Namubiru and Busungu, thousands of grandparents are left to bring up the children in the district. Since the first case of AIDS in Uganda was diagnosed in 1982 in Kasensero, a trading post on the shores of Lake Victoria, the disease has spread all over the country.

According to President Yoweri Museveni, between one to three million Ugandans could be HIV positive, while children orphaned by the scourge have shot up to one million. All that these children have known in their short lives is sickness, funerals and almost constant mourning. It is a traditional belief in Uganda that if an orphan is abandoned, then the ghosts of the dead will haunt the clan. So, usually the grandparents or the clanspeople take charge of orphans. But of late, this traditional system is being stretched to its limits and Ugandans are beginning to fear a breakdown of the extended family system.

A UNICEF statistician, Susan Hunter, puts the number of AIDS orphans in Rakai at 25,000. Others say the figure is too conservative. Emmanuel Pinto, a member of parliament from the same district, who organised a head count in 1990, claims there are at least 40,000 orphans in Rakai. Health experts say that the transmission rate of AIDS from infected mothers to their children is between 30-40 per cent. However, there are no records showing when the mother died or how old the children were when she contracted the disease. It is, therefore, not known how many of the surviving orphans in Rakai — or, indeed, in Uganda — are infected by the virus. As a result, there is now a stigma attached to the AIDS orphans and an increasing reluctance, on the part of potential caretakers, to look after them.

Pinto recalls a group of orphans his team found, five siblings under the care of a 17-year-old. "They used to cook in an old paint can, as their property and all their possessions were taken over by relatives," he says. And as a villager, Samson Mukabya comments, these children, burdened with an immense responsibility, turn cynical and bitter. "We have lost many of our teenagers to the Lake (Victoria), where they get casual jobs from fishermen. Growing up without school or a vocational education, these children are potential rebels. What is their future ? What is ours?" asks he.

The orphans' future can, at best, be uncertain, but their present situation is much like that of 14-year-old John Lumanzi. He ran away from his uncle's house in the neighbouring district of Masaka, three years ago, because he "was being treated very badly". When he reached the shores of Lake Victoria, he began peddling whatever came his way, and helping out the fishermen whenever they had some work. He now lives alone in a tiny shack he has built quite close to the shore. Similarly, many girls escape from abusive guardians. It is believed that the influx of teenage barmaids at Rakai's main town, Kyotera, are AIDS orphans who have escaped from their caretakers.

It is the future of such children that worries both local as well as international agencies. For instance, Pinto formed the Rakai Development Association which pays the orphans' school fees that their guardians cannot afford. He was also instrumental in forming the Uganda Community-Based Association for Children, which is a national body assisting all children in difficult circumstances. New classrooms have been added to Rakai's Luganzo Primary School, and a day-care centre meant for 30 children (but which currently accommodates 50), was also started. Pinto, who insists that the orphans should remain within their community, is also working out the legalities of demarcating an overgrown plantation into plots, to give out to jobless, teenaged boys.

With the AIDS scourge escalating rapidly, the Uganda AIDS Commission (funded by UN agencies and the US) was set up in 1991 to coordinate the efforts of various concerned groups. It will strive to control and prevent the spread of the disease. Among the Commission's many technical sub-committees is one that deals with AIDS orphans, chaired by Jolly Nyeko, senior probation and welfare officer in the ministry of labour and social welfare. Nyeko says that her ministry is extremely concerned as the disease hits the most productive segment of the country the hardest. And one of the government's priorities on this, according to her, is to disseminate information on the proper care of the orphaned children.

"We stress community-based action and we encourage proper standards of children's care, especially the legal aspect. These children have to be protected because they stand to lose their property," she explains. Nyeko points out that inheritance customs permit the dead man's brothers to claim his property, leaving his widow and children in the lurch.

"We are speaking out in order to create awareness among grassroots leaders so that they can protect widows and children. We are also concerned with child abuse from relatives of the orphans," says Nyeko. There are many instances of orphans who are taken into a relative's home and are then denied basic rights, according to Nyeko. "They are made to slave for the family that takes them on," she says.

While the government encourages foster care and adoption, it concedes that it is not easy, particularly since Ugandan laws have strict rules on adoption. Rev. Dr. Tom Tuma, the programme officer with the behavioural and social coordination at the Uganda AIDS Commission, suggests that taking into consideration the government's policy of looking after or-phans within their communities, there must be an outside group to supervise guardians. Concerned people are urging the church to help out. "Customarily, the responsibility of caring for orphans and widows falls on the church. Therefore we should build on this," says Tuma.

ZAMBIA

Sewing up a new business
Colleen Lowe Morna

Lusaka — Sewing for a living is not uncommon among African women. But mending jute grain bags — as Maryanne Ng'uni does — is certainly an unusual variation on the theme. In her two-roomed quarters on the outskirts of Lusaka, Ng'uni salvages old, imported grain bags by cutting a handful of used bags to patch the others, using heavy duty sewing machines. After a year in business, she has managed to repay all her debts and triple her own income. She has also become a popular figure among farmers who can now get vital grain bags on time, and at a quarter of the previous price. Most important, last year Ng'uni saved the Zambian government US$ 360,000 in scarce foreign exchange. That is set to rise even more, as this simple, yet energetic Zambian businesswoman plans to ex-pand her present business, and go into the actual production of grain bags, using local materials.

"The begining is always a bit difficult," Ng'uni reflects modestly, "but I think I've broken through now, and I never want to look back again."

Ng'uni owes her sucess to a combination of creativity and determination. Previously, she worked for a bank for 18 years, rising from the position of clerk to accountant. At 39, Ng'uni decided to leave the job and go into business.

"I took early retirement because I wanted to do something

that my children could fall back on, if they could not get jobs in the formal sector," says Ng'uni, whose three daughters range in age from seven to 18. "At the same time," she adds, "I wanted to help young boys and girls who could not get very far in their education."

Initially, Ng'uni set her sights on making sack-covered water cooler bags, used by many who cannot afford refrigerators in hot, developing countries. But she ran into a snag : although she could get the canvas and old sacks locally, she would have to import the cork top. Her investigations led to another idea why not mend and resell the grain bags themselves?

In Zambia, as in many African countries which do not grow jute, ensuring an adequate supply of grain bags during the harvest season is a perennial problem. Zambia imports some 20 million bags annually, at a cost of about a dollar a bag. Apart from the transportation problems faced by this landlocked country, the grain bag imports are a substantial drain on the foreign currency reserves in a country which only earns some US$ 700 million annually from its exports, and has a debt burden close to US$ seven billion.

Ironically, in Zambia as elsewhere in Africa, grain bags are used only once and then discarded, many with just a hole or two. Applying a principle well known to many mothers who patch their children's clothes, Ng'uni found she could salvage upto 2,000 bags. With the help of the Parastatal Small Industries Development Organisation (SIDO), Ng'uni wrote up a project proposal for presentation to the African Commercial Bank. She had to give most of her gratuity as a down payment on the loan. "But I had done my homework well, and I was sure the project would succeed," says the middle-aged woman.

It was a good bet. Soon after receiving the loan, Ng'uni travelled to the U.K. to buy six sewing machines. She signed on 27 school leavers — boys and girls — to work a 24-hour shift, and made arrangements with farmers' organisations to regularly collect old grain bags and supply them with refurbished ones.

Operations began in January last year. During the first year, Ng'uni mended 360,000 grain bags, each one saving a dollar for the government. She sells them back to the farmers at about 25 cents each — a quarter of what they would pay to buy new ones.

Ng'uni has repaid her entire loan, met her labour and overhead costs and managed to make a profit of three times the wage she earned at the bank. But Ng'uni does not dismiss her earlier banking experience. "As a banker, you are always looking ahead. I remember once I had to open a branch for my bank and it was always in the red. Eventually, the manager and myself figured out a way of getting the branch back into credit. From then, we never looked back," recalls Ng'uni.

The fear of taking risks, which is one of the biggest deterrents for small entrepreneurs, is one which Ng'uni has evidently conquered. She is presently negotiating further finance to import ten new sewing machines and a truck through US Aid Commodity Import Scheme, whereby entrepreneurs can pay the sum in local currency in Zambia, and receive the equivalent in foreign exchange in the USA. The Zambian businesswoman plans to move to larger premises in the industrial sites, in order to expand the scope of her business. She also wants to make new bags, using a locally grown material called kenaf, currently being experimented with in Zambia.

"But I still haven't given up the idea of water bags," she says. She has approached Zambia's Scientific Research Council to see if they can come up with a substitute for cork. "If that can be solved, I will definitely make water bags," she says resolutely.

Easing women's work
Zarina Geloo

Lusaka — Finding clean water used to be a major chore for Jaliana Mwaanga. "The nearest taps to my village are only ten minutes away, but they've been broken for the past two years," she says. "I sometimes walked for an hour before I could get to a working tap to draw clean water."

Mwaanga, who lives in Chipepo village, about 20 kms from Lusaka, is a widow with five children. She used to make three trips a week to the distant tap and her two eldest children, 12 and 11 years old, helped carry the load.

But that was before she learned how to make a simple water purifier from a few inexpensive materials. Now Mwaanga, who earns her livelihood selling vegetables in the local market, no longer treks the long distance for drinking water. Instead, she draws water from a shallow stream near her home, passes it through her homemade water purifier, and has clean water for the day.

Instruction on how to build a water purifier is part of a rural education programme started in 1980 by the local YWCA. The process is unbelievably simple. A clay pot is filled first with stones, then with charcoal and topped with sand. Stream water is poured in through the top and impurities are removed as the water filters through. Clean water is dispensed through a nozzle fixed at the bottom of the pot.

Spending less time searching for clean water means that Mwaanga's mornings have been freed for other household chores that were usually left until her day was over at the market. "We do not have much as far as technology goes, so most of our work must be done manually," she says. "If someone teaches us ways of easing our burden for free, we certainly appreciate it." The women have also been taught to make clay or cement pots which can each store 35 litres of water.

The water purifier is just one of many labour-saving items that the YWCA has taught village women to make during workshops conducted in rural Zambia by the organization's 16 branches. Spreading the word about appropriate technology — a catchword for devices that are suitable in rural setting — is a major focus of the YWCA in Zambia. It is part of their wider programme to promote primary health care, proper nutrition and basic literacy in rural communities.

"We decided on appropriate technology specifically for women to ease their workload," says Angela Mavunga, a YWCA project organizer. It is becoming common, especially in rural areas, to find women overburdened, taking care of household chores even as they go out and earn the family income. And what is special about appropriate technology, as Mavunga explains, is that "nothing new or expensive goes into making the devices. Everything is cheap and locally available."

Another example of labour-saving devices the women have learned to make are basket cookers, which Mavunga says have become popular even in urban areas. The basket cooker is made from a straw basket or bucket. The outer portion is covered with hay, waste cotton or grass for insulation. A sack or cloth is tightly bound to the outside of the bucket to hold the insulation in place. A tightly-fitted lid is similarly insulated. A sand-filled dish is then put under the bottom of the basket, and whenever food needs to be cooked or warmed, a red-hot brick is placed in the sand. The pot is set on the brick and the food inside can then be left to stew.

The basket cooker has transformed Lukwesa Malama's life. "It was one mad rush. From the fields I would hurry home to put a meal together before the children started crying for food", she recalls. Now she leaves her stews cooking slowly in the basket. When she returns home in the evening, the stew is done and ready to eat with nshima, a staple food of thick corn porridge.

The cooker has done for Malama what the water purifier did for Mwaanga: provide a lot of extra time. "And the children are now much happier and the house much cleaner because of the extra time I have for them," she says.

Among the other inexpensive labour-saving devices that the YWCA has taught women to make are ventilated pit latrines, water coolers, brick stoves and corn shellers. It has also started some income-generating programmes in several rural Zambia provinces. Women in some communities make ceramic items and weave cloth and in other villages, craft jewellery and dolls.

Before a project is started, the YWCA questions residents about their needs, says Ruth Thiessen, YWCA co-ordinator. "If getting clean water is a problem, we teach them to make water filters and clay pots for purifying and storing water. If it is hygiene, we begin with ventilated pit latrines and give primary health talks," she says.

As 23-year-old Irene Chisupa can tell you, her children are now healthy because she attended YWCA's talks on nutrition and basic health care. Indeed, hundreds of rural Zambian women like Chisupa, who were married when they were almost children themselves and knew little about childcare, feel deeply indebted to the YWCA's myriad projects. Their children now eat balanced, healthy meals and are immunised against dreaded diseases.

Inventing for self-reliance

Tiza Banda

Lusaka — News that Mary Chilufya had invented a traditional incubator using cheap local raw materials, spread like wild fire. A Zambian flying doctor service team and the Zambian health minister, Roger Sakhuka, flew to see the invention in Chilufya's village, Mansa, near the Zambian-Zairean border. The incubator had been used twice to keep premature babies alive until they reached normal weight.

In the past, premature babies often died because they did not get to the local hospital, 250 kms away, in time. Villagers used to cycle to the district hospital to seek assistance as there are no ambulances in the area. "Something had to be done to save these innocent lives," said Chilufya, a woman in her early 40s with little formal education. "This idea came to me and I'm glad it worked."

Chilufya used clay for the base where the baby lies. Reeds provided small windows, sisal was used for warmth and the legs of the incubator she made from bamboo. The incubator, made such an impact that Zambia's president, Kenneth Kaunda, called on non-governmental organisations and research institutions to promote more appropriate technology. Two months later, the University of Zambia, the United Nations Children's Fund (UNICEF), the Norwegian Agency for Development (NORAD) and other NGOs organised a fair where people could display their appropriate technology devices. Over 40 women participants from rural and urban areas attended the fair. A committee, made up of the fair's organisers, selected the incubator, a charcoal refrigerator and a wooden pump for national promotion.

In selecting the refrigerator, Isabel Musuku, a committee member and national president of the Young Women's Christian Association (YWCA) explained that most people in the rural areas do not have electricity. Although the government has started a rural electrification programme it needs over US$ one billion to complete the project. And even if electricity does come to the villages, most Zambians earn an average of about R 400 kwacha (US$ 50) a month, and cannot afford to buy electric refrigerators. Whereas in parts of the north-western province, a co-operative of 10 women sells charcoal refrigerators for only 40 kwacha (US$ 5).

By promoting these items, said Rao Sayu of the Mount Mukula Research Centre, "women can keep their food and milk cool without being millionaires." Thirty-six-year-old Dorothy Mutale who made the charcoal refrigerator, said that one major problem with the fridge is that it has to be kept continuously cool by sprinkling water on the charcoal, but she hopes that a research centre will improve on this. Mutuale, a primary school teacher, has also formed a women's club interested in making alternative technology devices in Chipata, in Zambia's eastern province.

The government also plans to encourage such community projects, said Zambia's minister of co-operatives, Justine Mukando. His ministry intends organising seminars on how to run them. The success of these projects has yet to be seen but at present, with this southern African country's economy in the doldrums, hope is being pinned on a new economic strategy.

Kaunda has already announced various changes in the government's policy to revamp the country's ailing economy. Zambia severed relations with the International Monetary Fund (IMF) and cancelled the foreign exchange auctioning system, pegging the country's currency at eight kwacha to the US dollar. The kwacha's fluctuating value had caused inflation and brought untold suffering to the low-paid Zambian worker.

By reducing the amount of money paid to the IMF to 10 per

cent of export earnings, Kaunda said the government will be able to concentrate more on internal development and investment. Internal development had almost reached stagnation and Zambians were losing their jobs every day because companies were forced to operate below capacity, sometimes at only 20 per cent. It is estimated that two million youth of the country's population of seven million, are currently unemployed.

Kaunda has called on the nation to be "creative" and start self-help projects because no "manna from heaven will feed them." In an effort to spread the appropriate technology nationwide, the government has made plans to have items exhibited at all provincial and district shows, and at the country's international trade fair to be held in the copperbelt.

Commerce and industry minister Jameson Kalauka is optimistic that these items will flourish. "Who knows, these devices, once improved upon and made in large quantities, could be exported to other under-developed nations. All Zambians need to put their heads together and work as a team on this."

ZIMBABWE

Women farmers lead the way
Colleen Lowe Morna

Harare — Each Monday and Thursday, two days normally set aside for rest in Zimbabwe's Zvimba area, 25 farmers sneak away to their group farming plot to put in a few extra hours of work. On a hectare of land donated by one of the members, the year old Zvichanaka Farmer's Group has moved swiftly ahead. Having already experimented with growing sunflowers and beans, it has also learnt how to keep farm accounts and save money, and is now looking for ways of getting around the transport problems that plague the area. The name "Zvichanaka" in the local Shona language means "everything will be okay". Rebecca Muvezwa, the widow who chairs the group, quips that in a few years time the group will certainly have to change its name to "Zvakanaka" — "everything is okay".

The Zvichanaka Farmer's Group is one of 130 such units initiated by a joint project of the Ministry of Community and Cooperative Development and Women's Affairs (MCCDWA), along with the United Nations Food and Agricultural Organization (FAO), to help strengthen the role of women farmers. "The tendency in development projects," explains FAO senior Project Adviser Kate Truscott, "has been to hive women off into marginal activities which reinforce their domestic role." While there is nothing wrong with the sewing and knitting clubs per se, the MCCDWA and FAO project stresses that "women are actually farmers" and that "their rightful place is in all mainstream activities," says Truscott.

According to MCCDWA Permanent Secretary Tendayi Bare, this is achieved by using the "group demonstration method" in which advice, training and inputs are provided to the group on a specified plot. "The idea is that women will then transfer the knowledge to their own plots," Bare explains. Although the project does not exclude male members, they are restricted to no more than 40 per cent of the total. The most important feature of the project, according to Truscott, is that by having equal access to knowledge and inputs, women learn to exercise new powers of equality and decision making. The five year project, costing 1.5 million US dollars, has now been running for three years.

As in the case of Zvichanaka, which used to be a women's sewing and knitting club, many of the groups were grafted onto existing organizations. The problem with the sewing club, according to Zvichanaka member Saniso Mashayamombe, was that "we got very little money for our work, and we wanted to know more about farming, which is the main activity for most of us". After learning of the MCCDWA/FAO project, one member donated land for the demonstration plot, and members donated one bag of maize each to pay for seeds and fertilizer, which are supplied at a 50 per cent discount. The 18 women members also decided at that point to invite men into their ranks.

"We did this because there are certain tasks like ploughing and fencing which are more easily done by men," explains Muvezwa. Although men comprise half of the eight member committee, it is significant enough in this conservative rural community that a woman — and a widow at that — is in the lead position.

D.K. Mashayamombe, Saniso's husband, says that before independence in 1980 it would have been inconceivable for men to join such a group. "In the past, it was always men who were the leaders. But now this government of ours has taught women how to take charge. So now we follow our wives to the groups." He confesses that it has been good for the men concerned. "If a woman leads a man," he laughs, "he doesn't go backwards. Men used to drink beer and mess around before."

This group certainly has no time for that. From the beginning, meetings were fixed for twice a week. Any member who fails to turn up without a good enough reason has to pay a fine of US$ 1.50. The reason, according to Muvezwa, is that, "we did not want some members benefitting from work done by others". Although there is no restriction on what crops to grow, Zvichanaka picked sunflower and beans — two potentially lucrative cash crops which they felt they needed to know more about. Having one regular meeting spot makes it easier for the agricultural demonstrator to reach several farmers at once, and the project ensures that members get the full benefits of government extension services. "Many of us used to think that sunflower was just a weed. We didn't bother to plant it in rows, to add fertilizer to the soil, or to keep it free of weeds while it was growing," recalls Zvichanaka Vice Chairman, Fabion Mashayamombe. The group experiment has proved what a dramatic difference correct procedures can make. According to Muvezwa, this year the group plot yielded 36 bags of sunflower, compared to the average, among members, of 6-12 bags a hectare. "This season when I grow my sunflower crop I will follow the correct methods and get an even better yield than the group," Mashayamombe notes.

For the next year, the group has already obtained a plot for vegetable gardening from local authorities. The members also intend to experiment with dairy farming, which is increasingly encouraged among small-scale farmers. From contributions made by members, as well as sales of sunflower seed, the group expects to have some US$ 1000 in the bank at the end of the month. The primary purpose is to save enough money to help alleviate the perennial problem of getting transport to the Grain Marketing Board depot 12 kms away. Although it would be virtually impossible for the group to save the US$ 30,000 necessary to buy a truck, members hope they might get a donor to provide matching funds.

In the interim, the group is using its strength in numbers to help negotiate a more efficient and reliable service from local transporters. They are more likely to be interested in a contract to transport the over 900 surplus bags of grain of the 25 members, than in their individual needs. This is what pulling together is all about, feels Saniso Mashayamombe. "As a group we can plan, and have the capacity to see our plans through in a way which an individual cannot," she notes.

Membership in the group also has remarkable impact on the confidence of the women involved. Says Muvezwa: "You can tell the difference between the members of our group and others from the way they walk, their knowledge, their ability to reason or argue. They are not shy and withdrawn like others". Saniso Mashayamombe, readily agrees. "These days," she laughs, "I can even tell my husband to stay at home and do the cooking while I go off to a training course."

Caterpillar cocktail ?
Nina Shapiro

Gokwe — Gokwe Hotel chef Jameson Chinyoka grills great steaks for his customers. But when he cooks for himself, he prefers a delicacy never seen on the hotel's menu: caterpillars. "They're nice, like prawns," says Chinyoka of the insects, which another woman describes as tasting "like meat". Still another connoisseur is convinced that prepared properly, caterpillars "cannot be distinguished from crayfish cocktail".

Whatever the taste, there is no denying the enormous popularity of caterpillars in this northwestern district of Zimbabwe — one of the least developed and highly forested areas in the southern African country. So popular are the insects that entrepreneurs have begun to market packaged bags of cooked caterpillars, with a 100 gms packet selling for around Zimbabwean dollar 1.60 (just under one US dollar) at local stores. "They are in such great demand," say Abraham Munakamwe, a trader for Red Star wholesalers, which distribute packaged caterpillars around Gokwe, "we're always running out of them." Indeed, on a recent visit, Red Star was completely out of stock.

A research study undertaken by Ruvimbo Chimedza, agricultural economics professor at the University of Zimbabwe, documents the widespread use of caterpillars and other insects in this area. Almost half of the Gokwe households surveyed consumed insects on a regular basis, according to the study, which is not only interesting for sociological reasons, but because it could have important ramifications for public food policies. Chimedza argues that insects, a rich source of protein, could play an important role in nutritional planning. They could be especially beneficial throughout the developing world, where, as in Gokwe, meat and other standard sources of protein are scarce.

The consumption of insects has been "grossly underestimated", contends Chimedza, because they are considered inferior foods. "Officially, no one wants to recognise that they are an important source of food," she says. As the primary managers of the family diet, women generally gather and prepare insects. Sometimes the women have a surplus, and then they sell the insects in the local markets or on the streets.

When caterpillar season begins in Gokwe, its abundant trees crawl with the yellow and black striped insects. In Gokwe Central, the district's main town, everyone seems to have bowlfuls of caterpillars, shrivelled and faded after being boiled and dried, which they will stock up for the days ahead.

Lois Gwapiri, returning from an early morning caterpillar-picking venture in the forest, demonstrates how to prepare the insects. "First you clean out the insides," she says, squeezing a green, mucous-like substance from a caterpillar. "Then you wash, cook and add some salt. After cooking, you put them in the sun. When dry, you eat them with sadza (the staple cornmeal porridge)."

But recipes differ to suit individual tastes. People add other ingredients to prepare special caterpillar dishes — onions, oil, tomatoes, peanut butter and the spicy piri-piri sauce. According to Chimedza's survey, the fancier dishes are eaten as a main meal, while simply prepared caterpillars — boiled and salted — are common snacks.

Although not as popular as caterpillars, other insects too are commonly consumed here, according to the findings. Among the other favourites are locusts, crickets and flying ants. One of the reasons that insect-consumption began in Gokwe households, is that people had difficulty getting meat and so used insects as substitutes. However, their obvious delight in caterpillars suggests that they are eaten for enjoyment and not merely as a last resort.

Insects are not only tasty, they are nutritious. Chimedza bemoans the lack of attention paid to insects by national food programmes, which rely mainly on agriculture. In Gokwe Central, however, health officials are promoting insects for their protein value. Gokwe Hospital advises new mothers to feed their babies with caterpillars and the women seem to be doing just that. Munakamwe at Red Star says he gets a lot of mothers asking for caterpillars.

Milton Chemhuru, a leading doctor at Gokwe Hospital, sees many malnourished children. "It's a big problem here. People get no meat, chicken, nothing. How can they afford it, when neither parent is working and there are 10 children to feed?" he asks. So he advises mothers to exploit other protein-rich sources, like rats, for instance. "I always tell them, if you can catch and eat rats, they're very nutritious."

But this sometimes creates environmental problems. Often,

entire fields are set on fire in the pursuit of rats. Moreover, the gathering of flying ants and crickets, which entails digging holes in the earth, contributes to soil erosion. Chemhuru recalls seeing riverbanks lined with holes in his hometown in central Zimbabwe where crickets are extremely popular.

The other stumbling block is pesticides. Although pesticides are used only in the more affluent areas, they do destroy many of these insects. As one of the farmers said, "Locusts have a very high protein level, but if they come in millions, they've got to be destroyed." And the most popular insect, which damages crops the least — the caterpillar — is also killed along with the locusts.

Most people claim that their caterpillar-gathering methods are harmless. However, a walk with five women catching caterpillars in Gokwe woods revealed just the contrary. When the women spotted a tall tree laden with the insects which, unfortunately, were too high for them to reach, they immediately pulled out an axe and started chopping the tree. As soon as the tree fell, the women swooped down on the branches and plucked out all the caterpillars. But Knowledge Matapi, one of the women, said she was not worried about the damage caused, for "We cut down trees very rarely."

Still, sooner or later, people will have to balance the harm caused by gathering insects with the benefits accrued from eating them. And the first step in solving problems associated with such consumption, argues Chimedza, is the recognition that it exists: "As long as insects are not recognised as part of the household diet of a community, who is going to formulate policies concerning alternate forms of household diets?"

S. & S.E. Asia

S. ASIA

THE S.ASIAN REGION, home to a fifth of the world's population, cradle of ancient civilisations and religions, rich in its multiplicity of cultures, languages and ethnic strains is, in economic terms, one of the poorest in the world.

The six countries of Bhutan, Bangladesh, India, Nepal, Pakistan and Sri Lanka vary enormously in size, geography and resources. The small landlocked kingdoms of Bhutan and Nepal, nestled in the Himalayan ranges, have populations of 1.4 million and 18 million, respectively. Sri Lanka, the island nation off the southernmost tip of the Indian subcontinent, houses 16.8 million. Pakistan and Bangladesh, at opposite ends of the peninsula, have populations of 116 million and 112 million, and giant India which spans most of the subcontinent, is home for a staggering 830 million in 25 states and seven territories, uneasily bound together by religious and cultural ties, yet widely different from each other.

Caught in poverty

The one stark reality which encompasses all of S. Asia is the poverty of its people. Geography and demography partly explain why some of these nations are trapped in poverty.

Mountainous Nepal, for example, supports one of the world's densest populations on its limited arable land; its farmers are being forced to cultivate marginal lands and cut down forests to survive. Bangladesh in the east has fertile land but a population density three times that of overpopulated India, and is prone to recurrent floods and cyclones.

Equally significant is the fact that in the post-colonial period (independence from British rule came for most of these countries after World War II) several of these countries have been ruled by dictatorial and corrupt governments, whether hereditary, elected or imposed. These rulers have failed to free the people from the abysmal levels of impoverishment exacerbated by colonial exploitation. As a consequence, annual per capita incomes in the region range from a mere US$ 179 in Nepal to US$ 370 in Pakistan.

Bhutan and Nepal have been ruled by feudal lords, Pakistan until recently, by a series of military rulers, Bangladesh by both elected and martial law governments, Sri Lanka has witnessed years of emergency rule, and even India, where governments have been elected every few years, has experienced an emergency. Ethnic unrest, communal and sectarian strife, pro-democracy and separatist movements and inter-country conflicts, including some wars, have disrupted economies and drained national exchequers.

Uneven capitalist development, experiments in mixed or state-run economies and the pressures of a global accumulation of capital, have drawn almost every country in S. Asia into a net of exploitative production and an increasing marginalisation of the poor and disadvantaged. Growth-oriented development policies in these transitional societies have led to a large-scale displacement of traditional life-styles and sources of livelihood, often leading to violent conflicts over resources.

Political upheavals

Politically, some countries in the subcontinent have undergone positive changes in recent years; Nepal, for instance, dominated for years by hereditary Rana rulers, was stirred by the winds of democracy in late 1990. The people's movement forced the King to hold an election for the first time in 32 years and a democratic government was established under a constitutional monarchy. In Bangladesh, again at the end of 1990, people took to the streets to demand democracy and ousted the military dictator, President H. M. Ershad. The subsequent elections ushered in a democratic government, led by Begum Khaleda Zia, widow of a former president and leader of the Bangladesh National Party.

Elsewhere in the region, political changes have not been so promising. Pakistan had earlier experienced a prolonged but suppressed democracy movement led by Benazir Bhutto of the Pakistan People's Party. After the sudden death of military ruler, General Zia-ul Haq, Bhutto won the elections held in November 1988. She faced strong opposition from right-wing forces, her government was dismissed in 1990 and she lost the subsequent election.

Sri Lanka has been grappling with severe problems on the political front, including a prolonged civil war and an internal insurrection. India witnessed several changes in government, in quick succession, to the detriment of its economy. Even tiny Bhutan, long a haven of peace, was rocked by ethnic riots in 1991 when it tried to curb the entry of Nepalis from across the border.

A fallout of unrest in the region is the huge outlays on defence by countries which can ill afford it. Pakistan, for instance, has a large, parasitical army that has held the country in its grip for years. In 1988 when the government undertook its adjustment programme, predictably, the budget deficit was met by cutting down on meagre development resources while defence expenditure remained high at 6.6 per cent of its Gross Domestic Product. Pakistan's outlays on education and health have been small — only half its children go to primary school, its literacy rate of 26 per cent is among the world's lowest and for rural women, it is an unbelievable 6 per cent.

Another consequence of conflicts in the region and around it has been the creation of huge numbers of refugees that have swarmed to camps in neutral or sympathetic countries. For instance, the prolonged war for control of Afghanistan brought 3.5 million refugees to Pakistan's North West Frontier Province and Baluchistan, fuelling social unrest in the area. The Sinhala-

Tamil conflict in Sri Lanka pushed a few million Tamils into seeking refuge across the Indian Ocean in India's Tamil Nadu. On its eastern border India has also had to cope with large numbers of Chakma refugees and students fleeing Myanmar's repressive military regime. And the Bhutanese-Nepalese conflict has sent thousands scurrying to camps in Nepal.

One major cause of unrest in S.Asia and its neighbouring countries has been the fact that even where governments have been democratically elected, they have rarely prioritised the basics of human survival: adequate food and shelter for their entire populations. Safe water, sanitation, health services and education still elude large sections of people in the region. UNDP's Human Development Index, which ranks countries according to the basic facilities they provide citizens, places Asian countries low on its scale. With the exception of Sri Lanka, these countries rank from 120 for Pakistan to 147 for Bhutan, out of 160 countries.

The overwhelming majority of Asians, 73 per cent, are rural. The region has a higher rural population than any other in the world. And of course most of them depend on agriculture for a living. Although villagers in most of these countries grow enough food to feed the population, the average daily calorie intake is inadequate — between 83 per cent to 94 per cent of what is recommended. Life expectancy at birth is 58.4 years, lower than that of any other region in the world except sub-Saharan Africa. Only 56 per cent of people have access to health services, 72 per cent to safe water and 16 per cent to sanitation; and only 46 per cent are literate.

For women the implications of living in such deprivation are horrific. Poverty and patriarchy (sanctioned by both Hinduism and Islam, the dominant faiths here, and also by Christianity) combine to perpetuate their subordinate status. Given limited resources, women get less of everything, be it food, medicine, clothing or schooling. Malnourished women who eat skimpy meals, have heavy workloads and early and frequent pregnancies, unattended by trained medical staff, produce low birth-weight babies, many of whom die in infancy. Maternal and infant mortality rates are high, and even where infant mortality has declined, morbidity persists.

In scarce-resource societies male children who can quickly bring in an income are considered an asset while female children are perceived as a burden. In India especially, the cultural preference for sons even drives many families to kill baby girls. Modern technologies such as amniocentesis and ultrasound tests are misused to detect female foetuses and selectively abort them. In other families slow neglect and malnutrition among baby girls takes its toll. Two years ago the regional grouping, South Asian Association for Regional Cooperation (SAARC) was alerted to the problem by UNICEF and other agencies and declared 1990 as the Year of the Girl Child, in an effort to improve the situation.

Cultural constraints on female mobility severely restrict Asian women's access to most productive resources, occupations and services. In the mountain kingdom of Nepal, for instance, female literacy is just 13 per cent, among males, 38 per cent. Inevitably, female-headed households — an increasing reality in the region — are among the poorest in Asia, a problem most governments are only now beginning to address.

But in at least one country of the region, the situation is refreshingly different. Sri Lanka, known worldwide for its tea, its gems and its natural beauty, spends a big chunk of its small resources on the social sector. Its health indicators rival those of many middle income countries: life expectancy is 70 years, infant mortality as low as 25 per thousand live births, and literacy rates as high as 88 per cent. An efficient school system and a countrywide public health network — and, in previous years, a large food subsidy — ensured the welfare of its citizens.

Sri Lankan women do not suffer from the same level of gender discrimination as their sisters in the region. An amazing 84 per cent of them are literate, 85 per cent receive formal schooling, and at secondary school level they usually make up more than half the class; and they have access to health facilities and to employment.

These heartening successes in the social sector are regrettably not matched by economic growth. Sri Lanka's large public sector, the biggest employer in the country, has over-extended itself while failing to promote growth and employment. Unrest among an educated labour force with high expectations fuelled the traditional ethnic rivalry between the Sinhala majority and the Tamil minority, and exploded in a debilitating civil war in the early 1980s. Meanwhile the Sri Lankan government faced another crisis when the left-wing Janatha Vimukthi Peramuna (JVP) led a country-wide insurrection. It was crushed; but the government has had to borrow heavily to finance the war, deal with the JVP and revitalise the economy.

Development for whom?

Unlike Sri Lanka, which at least made attempts to give its people a reasonable standard of living, the development path followed by other governments in the region was modelled on borrowed western paradigms and took insufficient account of the needs of their people. Over the past four decades Asian countries have, with varying degrees of success, built up an infrastructure for industrialisation, improved agrarian technologies and created a growing service sector. In the process they have mostly neglected rural people, fostered large, inefficient bureaucracies and created prosperous elite and middle class urban groups who are cornering and consuming most of their countries' resources.

Liberal public spending, inefficient economies, large populations, ethnic and inter-country conflicts, social inequities, political opportunism, the inequities of international trade, dependence on imports like oil and expensive western technologies are among the many factors that have contributed to the crises now being faced by these countries. By the 1980s most S.Asian governments were faced with huge foreign debts and, forced to restructure their economies under pressure from the World Bank, IMF and other lending institutions.

Among the first to initiate stabilisation policies was Bangladesh, a country whose government depends heavily on foreign aid to keep going. Its fiscal debt was an incredible US$

11.3 billion at the end of 1990. Only the fact that the bulk of this debt is contracted on highly concessionary terms keeps this low-lying country's head above water. Neighbouring Nepal, like Bangladesh one of the poorest countries in the world, began making structural adjustments in 1987 and has increased its foreign exchange reserves, but it still depends heavily on concessional aid to fuel its economy. In June 1990 its foreign debt was US$ 1.5 billion.

Sri Lanka, which was unique in the region for its achievements in health, education and food has, since 1978, been under pressure from the IMF to cut back on public services. It began an abortive structural adjustment programme in late 1986; the effort was resumed by a new government in 1989, and currently, war-torn Sri Lanka requires foreign financing to the tune of US$ 900 million annually for development plans and balance of payments support.

Pakistan adopted a three-year adjustment programme in July 1988 but implementation has lagged and balance of payments assistance been delayed as a result, creating a problem for its government. And, most recently India, which for years resorted to deficit financing to support its development programme, was forced by a hard currency crisis in 1991 to adopt an aid and adjustment package.

The consequences of these radical shifts are only now becoming evident, as governments privatise industry, disinvest in public sector enterprises, reduce public spending, and cut subsidies in various sectors. One short term result is further unemployment in countries where unemployment and underemployment are chronic. Another is cuts in pre-shrunk budgets for social spending. This means less money for schooling, for public health services, for essentials like clean water, toilets and sanitation facilities.

The resource crunch also means there is less food on the poor person's plate. In Sri Lanka, for instance, the cuts in subsidies on wheat, rice and fertiliser pushed up food prices sharply. Sri Lanka's food subsidy in real value terms fell from a level of 100 in 1980 to 42 in 1985. Though a food stamp scheme provides some relief to low income groups, many, particularly plantation workers, now eat less. In the long term, the social instability that will result from the impact of all these threatens to rip apart the fabric of community life, making for an intensification of conflict within and between classes, communities, and ethnic and religious groups.

Environmental shock

To meet foreign debts governments are pushing export-led growth. One consequence will be the further erosion of the resource base of ordinary people. More forests will get cut down so that timber can be exported, more cash crops will be substituted for grain for home consumption, more seas and rivers will be fished for prawn, shrimp and other delicacies to export to the developed world. Intensive exploitation of natural resources will further degrade the environment of countries where exploding populations are already over-stretching available resources.

Intensive cash cropping, for instance, may lower the water table in an area, forcing farmers to invest resources in digging deeper and deeper tubewells to find the elusive water, until the point when it becomes uneconomical. Cash cropping could also mean problems of waterlogging or contamination by fertilisers and pesticides. Accelerating exports of commodities can have severe consequences on whole communities. For instance, in its desperate bid to push up exports, the Indian government permitted large scale export of cotton yarn. Exports rose from 40 million kgs in 1987-88 to over 100 million kgs in 1990-91; the result was that thousands of handloom weavers in a country famous for its centuries old textile industry were rendered unemployed and destitute. At the end of 1991 at least 73 starvation deaths among weavers in Andhra Pradesh in south India were reported in the press, over a period of just two months.

This stark example is only one of many such. In recent decades hundreds of communities have been marginalised by the 'advance' of development. Traditionally, the landless poor have depended on village common lands for sustenance, using these to graze cattle or gather fuelwood or simply as space for carrying on various occupations. The forests have been another source of sustenance, providing fuelwood, grass and leaves for fodder, fruits and roots for food, herbs for medicine, wood and bamboo for housing, wild grasses for making baskets or rope and even fresh wood for the datun, the indigenous herbal toothbrush. But the commons have increasingly been encroached upon by the village elite and the forests taken over by government forest departments. Recently, India's Minister for Environment went a big step further by offering developed countries and their multinational representatives 50 million hectares of so-called 'wasteland' (which is basically, village commons) in India for afforestation, to make up for the pollution their industries are causing to the earth's atmosphere.

For the villager, being deprived of rights to village commons and forests can be disastrous. When an earthquake devastated north India's hill districts of Uttarkashi and Tehri Garhwal in 1991, destroying homes and fields, shivering villagers camped out in rain and snow, unable to rebuild houses. Wood is the traditional building material in the area but the villagers dared not cut down trees from the forests, since that would mean breaking the law. Yet forest departments systematically sell tonnes of timber and permit contractors to fell whole forests, legally or illegally. India is losing 2.3 per cent of its forest cover annually, neighbouring Nepal loses 4 per cent each year.

Governments face international pressure to enforce conservation of forest flora and fauna. The demands of foreign and domestic tourism have prompted the declaration of many forest areas as wildlife and bird sanctuaries and parks. In the process forest dwellers face eviction from their villages. Others living near parks and sanctuaries face constant danger from animals they dare not attack or kill because the animals are protected by law. It is paradoxical that the life of a wild elephant or tiger is worth more than human life, as people discover when they get meagre compensation from the government for the loss of a loved one.

When tribals or other forest dwellers are denied traditional user rights to forest produce, confrontations are inevitable. In Saharanpur, in north India, for instance, villagers used to freely

gather a type of forest grass which they twined into rope for
sale. The forest department took over that right and now sells
the grass through its depots. Members of ropemakers' cooperatives are militantly struggling for a restoration of their
traditional user rights to the forest. Some years ago, villagers
who were refused access to the Bharatpur bird sanctuary,
again in north India, set part of it on fire as a protest, and there
are many such instances from different parts of the subcontinent.

Rural environments are also being degraded as industry
invades newer areas. Huge plants are sited on village lands and
meagre compensation given to owners. Jobs are promised but
villagers rarely have the requisite skills, so that ultimately
outsiders benefit. The factories want only discharge effluents
into rivers, polluting people's major source of drinking water
and poisoning flora and fauna. Farmers sometimes find their
land degraded and their livelihood lost, and fisherfolk can no
longer fish the rivers.

Even the building of a road or bridge in a remote area has
all sorts of unexpected and often adverse consequences. While
access to schools, hospitals and markets becomes easier,
villages get integrated into the larger economy and village
produce is sent to distant cities. For the producer, this may
mean a higher cash income but, inevitably, prices of all
produce grown in the area go up too. Village children get less
milk, vegetables, eggs and other food and the little cash saved
goes to buy consumer goods like a watch or a radio. For the
poorest in the villages, who survived on the largesse of richer
folk who grew more than they could consume, there is now
no surplus — it is all sold for cash.

The exodus

Driven to the wall, marginalised rural people have only two
options: to agitate or migrate. Migration has been the traditional response. Millions of rural people have migrated to towns
and cities in search of employment. Between 1960 and 1990
S.Asia's urban population grew from 17 per cent to 27 per cent.

In India, Bombay and Calcutta, in Nepal, Kathmandu, in Bangladesh, Dhaka, in Pakistan, Karachi, and other cities are terribly overcrowded. They reflect urban chaos at its worst, with shortages of all civic amenities, from housing to drinking water, public toilets, buses and trains, hospitals, telephones, gas connections and other necessities.

As unemployment in the cities mounts, the urban option is drying up. The alternative has been to migrate to other countries, within the region and beyond it. Several nations in the developed world, such as the U.S., Canada, Britain and Germany have substantial Asian populations. With the developed countries increasingly discouraging immigration from the Third World, Asians have found other avenues: during the past decade, there has been a mass migration of labour, mostly unskilled and semi-skilled, to oil-rich West Asia. For hard currency-strapped governments, remittances sent home by foreign workers were a much needed bonus: Bangladesh, for instance, received remittances of US$ 761 million in 1990 — an amount equal to 20 per cent of its imports.

In patriarchal cultures migration tends to be primarily male and families are usually left behind, making for more and more female-headed households. In countries which send large numbers of labourers abroad, the psychological and cultural consequences are slowly coming to the fore. In India's southern state, Kerala, from which several million have migrated, Indian psychiatrists have observed what they label the 'Gulf syndrome' : increased mental stress among the wives of Gulf workers. In Sri Lanka the patttern has been the reverse; when Kuwait was invaded, there were some 90,000 Sri Lankan workers in the country and a phenomenal 80 per cent of them were women who worked as domestics in rich Kuwaiti homes. Sri Lankan social workers report a high incidence of juvenile delinquency among children left behind by these poor migrant women workers.

Most tragic of all has been the migration of masses of women from Nepal's picturesque but poor mountain villages to the brothels of Indian cities like Bombay. Many are lured out of their homes with promises of marriage or a well-paid job in

Kathmandu, and sold to flesh traders. Others volunteer to go, driven by hunger and deprivation. There are an estimated 200,000 Nepali women in Indian brothels, many of them as young as ten years. Economic migration is chronic in countries like Nepal and Bangladesh; migrants often swamp indigenous populations, leading to political unrest. India, where per capita incomes are higher, has faced many waves of immigration from these countries. In the Indian state of Sikkim, people of Nepali origin out number the Sikkimese, and in the state of Assam migrants from Bangladesh skewed the population pattern, sparking off an Assamese nationalist movement and an anti-foreigner agitation.

Internal migration from village to city has of course been an age old phenomenon, aggravated by the uneven development of different regions. Several hill districts of India, for example, are 'money-order economies', dependent on remittances from male migrants. Women bear the burden of working the fields, gathering fuelwood from degraded forests, fetching drinking water from distant springs, foraging fodder for the cattle, cooking, rearing children and nursing the sick and old.

A second option for marginalised people is agitation, and the S.Asian region has seen many small and big struggles of marginalised people, tribals, dalits (lower castes in India), religious and ethnic minorities. It is the survival struggles of marginalised people like these which many WFS features highlight, whether they are individual stories of ragpicking children in the cities who survive on the scraps they find on garbage heaps, or the militant struggles of tribals threatened by displacement because of the building of giant dams like the Narmada Sagar in India or the Mahaweli in Sri Lanka, or the peaceful, purposeful struggles of women's groups to organise urban and rural women around issues of domestic violence and rape which threaten their very lives.

S. E. ASIA

Sheer diversity marks this region of countries known as much for its wealth as for its appalling poverty. On the one hand is the small city state of Singapore, whose human development indicators rank it among the developed countries of the world; on the other are war-ravaged countries like Kampuchea where life is as unpredictable as the next landmine burst. Hongkong, Singapore, South Korea and Taiwan are S.E. Asia's four little dragons, newly industrialised countries known for the economic miracles their people have worked. Neighbouring them are nations struggling for political and economic democracy like Thailand, Malaysia, Indonesia and the Philippines.

Not unexpectedly, it is this group of countries that has witnessed amazing struggles by resilient, resourceful women and men to cope with adverse economic and political conditions, and it is here that many radical initiatives have been taken to place environmental concerns on national and international agendas.

In terms of size, numbers and topography these countries vary. Thailand lies on the south-eastern end of the vast Asian continent, with a leg stretching into the Gulf of Siam. Beyond lies Malaysia, stretched along the peninsula upto Singapore and then across the sea to its two provinces of Sabah and Sarawak on the island of Borneo. The rest of Borneo, now known as Kalimantan, falls into Indonesian territory as do the large islands, Sumatra and Java, and numerous others dotted across the seas. Up north lies the Philippines, sprawled over 7100 islands.

In terms of population, Malaysia has only 18 million residents, Thailand 55 million, the Philippines 62 million and Indonesia a phenomenal 184 million — the world's fifth largest population. The majority of people in these countries, as in S.Asia, are rural, with 57 per cent of Malaysians and Filipinos living in the villages, followed by 69 per cent of Indonesians and 77 per cent of Thais.

Unlike the extreme poverty of S.Asia, however, these nations, measured by the world human development index, fall into the medium development category, with the exception of Indonesia which offers low human development opportunities to its people. Per capita incomes range from a high US$ 2320 in Malaysia to a low US$ 500 in Indonesia. Life expectancy in S.E.Asia as a whole is 62 years, calorie intake is an average 111 per cent, 72 per cent have access to health services, 47 per cent to safe water, 57 per cent to sanitary facilities, and the adult literacy rate is 82 per cent.

Its history & economy

Historically, the area now comprising Malaysia, Singapore, Indonesia, Borneo, southern Thailand and the Philippines was known as the larger Malay archipelago, with a Malay socio-cultural world of its own, before colonisation began in the sixteenth century. The European powers introduced new political boundaries, new settlements, new modes of agriculture, and transformed the economy and ecology of their colonies. To meet the raw material needs of their industries, they exploited the fields, mines and forests of the region, cutting down precious timber resources and replacing tropical forests with rubber plantations, just as they had introduced indigo cultivation in India and tea in Sri Lanka.

Prized for spices and other natural resources, the Malay peninsula and the Indonesian islands were, between the sixteenth and eighteenth centuries, fought over by local sultans, Portuguese, Dutch and British traders. In 1824 the British and Dutch agreed to split this composite area, bound by the Islamic faith, cultural tradition and language, into two: the British got Malaya and the Dutch took present-day Indonesia. Various Malay sultanates became British 'protectorates'.

Modern Malaysia is a federation of sultanates but real power is controlled by the leader of the majority party in an elected parliament. Many of Malaysia's political problems today stem from the fact that it is a multi-racial nation. Its ethnic composition is no accident of history; it was engineered by the British to suit their economic interests. Chinese were brought in to work the tin mines and Indians to labour on the rubber plantations. This policy gradually transformed the ethnic, demographic and economic pattern of the area, making postcolonial Malaysia (independence was negotiated as late as 1957) a volatile state, riven by class and ethnic conflict.

In 1965 Singapore withdrew from the Malaysian federation and used its geographic advantage as a port to grow into a small, rapidly developing country with a highly educated and productive workforce. Indonesia, fought over by Spanish, Portuguese, Dutch and British interests, was ruled for over a century by the Dutch until it finally achieved independence in 1954. The country was led by the nationalist leader, Sukarno, until the 1965 coup by General Suharto whose prolonged regime has given the country stability at the cost of democracy. Revolts by students and militant Muslim groups have been crushed but unrest simmers.

Thailand, proud of the fact that it is the only country in the region which was never colonised is, paradoxically, subject to more intense neo-colonial domination than any other nation in the region. Since 1946, when a pro-American monarch was installed on the throne, the country has been under American influence. In 1961 American troops entered the country to curb an insurrection in neighbouring Laos; they stayed for 14 years and left a deep scar on Thai society. Today Thailand is ruled by a constitutional monarchy with the trappings of parliamentary democracy but real power vests with the army, backed by American support. In recent decades it has been subject to a series of coups, attempted or accomplished, and has also witnessed protests for democracy.

The Philippine archipelago of 7100-odd islands was given a name and unity by sixteenth century Spanish invaders who ruled it until 1898 when they ceded it to the U.S. In 1946 the Philippines was declared independent, but was ruled by feudal elites for years. In the last two decades, it has seen dictatorial, martial rule as well as a sustained democratic struggle which succeeded in bringing about a popular uprising, followed by free elections. Grassroots militancy and an extraordinary degree of political maturity and mobilisation, distinguishes the Philippines from its neighbours.

In terms of their economies, these countries are endowed with rich natural resources. Indonesia has a well developed agrarian economy, plentiful primary energy resources, mineral deposits and timber resources. In the Seventies oil and gas exports kept the economy buoyant, but when oil and commodity prices dipped in the Eighties, the government devalued the currency and restructured the economy, diversifying the economic base. Textile and timber industries, among others, have grown rapidly in the Eighties.

Malaysia, with impressive resources of cultivable land, oil and gas, rubber, tin, timber, palm oil and cocoa, has averaged a 6.4 per cent growth rate annually for the last 20 years. But even Malaysia's abundant resources have their limits — forest cover has been reduced and the government has had to restrict logging in the peninsula.

By contrast the Philippines remains incredibly poor — in 1988 about half the population was below the poverty line. In the past decade over a million workers, a large number of them women, have emigrated, mostly to work as labourers in the Gulf countries or as domestics in Europe, the U.S. and Hongkong. After Corazon Aquino came to power in 1986, the government struggled towards economic recovery and initiated stabilisation and structural adjustment programmes, supported by the IMF and other creditors. The Gulf crisis cost the Philippines a US$ 50 million decline in workers' remittances from the region while the cost of oil imports rose by US$ 400 million.

Thailand's central plains grow rice in plenty and it is the world's largest rice exporter; but its economy is rapidly moving from being agro-based to industrial. Manufacturing and the service sector are growing and the textile industry in particular is booming. The focus is on export-led industrial growth, which is expected to solve the employment problem. In 1990 Thailand's GDP growth rate was over 10 per cent.

Development policies followed by these countries have

favoured certain groups at the expense of others. In Malaysia, for example, the ruling party has aggressively pursued a pro-Malay policy to curb the Chinese, and Indians have been neglected or discriminated against in the process. Many Indians still work on the rubber and oil-palm plantations in conditions of abject misery. In Indonesia, where there is a population imbalance, with the majority concentrated in Java and two small adjacent islands, the government tried to resettle people on distant islands, forcing tribals and indigenous peoples out of their homelands. The largest ever colonisation scheme in history, funded by the World Bank and foreign companies, has caused untold human suffering and the loss of two million hectares of prime forest. Nearly a million people are to be moved into West Papua whose indigenous population is less than a million.

Escalating development, dwindling resources

The rapid destruction of the forests of the region, especially in Malaysia and Indonesia which were once blessed with immense forest resources, is a major issue for environmentalists and non-governmental organisations alike. Malaysia exports two-thirds of the world's tropical logs, destroying 700,000 hectares of forest annually.

A third of the forests in the Malaysian province of Sarawak have been logged, depriving forest dwellers of their primary resource. But when they organise to protest, they face the wrath of the timber lobby. In September 1989, for example, the Penan people of Sarawak barricaded roads to stop lorries from taking away timber; large numbers were jailed by the government.

Much of this destruction has been caused by multinationals. Recently, the American Scott Paper Company, which makes the popular Scotties Tissues, leased 80,000 hectares of rainforest in Irian Jaya, to log the forest and plant eucalyptus trees for use by a woodchip, pulp and paper mill that it planned to set up. A sustained campaign by local and foreign NGOs calling for boycott of company products, and pressure on the government by aid agencies forced the company to jettison its US$ 650 million project.

First World companies destroy Third World forests on the one hand, while dictating reforestation strategies on the other. Thai NGOs are currently campaigning against the award of a reforestation consultancy contract to the Finnish company, Jaako Poyry, which has similar contracts in the Philippines, Sri Lanka, Nepal, Kenya and Tanzania. Thai environmentalists say the company is unfamiliar with local needs and its programme is geared solely to growing trees for the wood industry.

Big dam projects that have come up in most Third World nations can be serious hazards, and invariably displace large populations, often of tribals and indigenous people. In Indonesia, inhabitants displaced by the Kedung Ombo Dam, financed by the World Bank, persisted in their demand for compensation for their land, and got it. But such cases are rare. More typical is the instance of the Batang Ai Dam in Sarawak, Malaysia, which displaced the Iban people. A researcher who visited a showpiece resettlement colony of 3000 Iban found that, while earlier, 90 per cent of families had owned over 10 acres of good rice land, they now own no rice land at all and are compelled to work on the government's rubber and cocoa plantations for below subsistence wages. Additionally, a good 60 per cent are well below the poverty line. Customarily, Iban women had equal rights to riceland and did most of the cultivating, yet compensation was paid to the men.

Thailand provides a classic lesson in maldevelopment. The government's pursuit of a rapid industrialisation policy proved extremely detrimental for agriculture, on which two-thirds of the people survive. Farmers failed to benefit from new technologies, while productivity was increased by hacking forests in order to bring more land under cultivation. Rivers were dammed to provide power for industry, leading to the displacement of many farmers. The landless were further marginalised as the rural environment became degraded. This clearing of land for agriculture, and illegal logging, reduced forests to 20 per cent of the total land area. It was in 1988, following floods caused by deforestation, that the government banned logging.

The landless had only one option: migration. Large numbers moved to Bangkok because industry and jobs were concentrated in the capital. Half of Thailand's factories and industrial estates are located here and in its vicinity, and 75 per cent of the country's two million tonnes of industrial waste are produced in Bangkok, making it an environmental nightmare.

In the Philippines, too, there have been moves in recent years to rapidly industrialise by borrowing funds from foreign agencies. The Filipino government has drawn up a 10-year billion peso industrialisation programme but is already facing problems of implementation. In southern Luzon, farmers are opposing the takeover of their lands for a hi-tech industrial zone; they say the zone will displace 4.4 million people but provide jobs only for 340,000. Meanwhile, on the political front, in a country of large feudal estates where two per cent of the people own 60 per cent of the land, but more than half the population are peasants, land reform still remains elusive.

Women resist

The implications for women of these emerging trends are complex and varied, depending on women's existing situation in their countries, explicit biases in development strategies, and the extent to which they reinforce patriarchal control. In Malaysia, for instance, Malay customary law recognised women's economic contribution and gave peasant women equal rights to possess and cultivate land. Today, although Malaysian village women control between 10-30 per cent of village lands, government policies continue to target land development schemes and provide agricultural training and credit to men, marginalising women's role. This particular bias on the part of governments, is evident across the region.

Nevertheless, the period since the Seventies has seen a widespread growth in women's consciousness regarding their oppression and its aggravation by inappropriate development policies. Women's groups have emerged to challenge and critique conventional wisdom on development, fight the ex-

ploitation of women in multinational factories, in free-trade
zones, against agricultural practice that harms them directly,
and against their commodification by the media and the sex-
tourism industry. In the Eighties, Malaysian women cam-
paigned on the issue of violence against their sex and
persuaded the government to amend the rape law; in 1989 the
government, which had ignored women in all its development
plans till then, brought out a National Policy on Women. In the
Philippines, women were in the forefront of the struggle to
oust the Marcos regime; years of political activity, whether in
the communist underground or through centrist politics,
church groups òr NGO activity, have steeled Filipinas into
demanding that their government implement more pro-peo-
ple and pro-women policies. Given their long tradition of community organising, Filipinas are acting in various ways to
improve their living standards and their environment, through
organising health workshops, improving sanitation in slums,
or forming cooperatives, organising credit and skill training
and starting ambitious self-employment ventures. Large
peasant women's groups are similarly questioning land
policies and the over-use of dangerous pesticides and fertilisers.

Both Filipinas and Thai women are organising to cope with
the special forms of degradation women face because of
poverty — sexual exploitation at work, prostitution (and its
often lethal corollary, AIDS) and the sale of women as 'mail
order brides' to men in the developed world. Cultural role
models and poverty make women specially vulnerable. In
Thailand, for instance, daughters are expected to look after
parents and family, even if they have to sell their bodies to do
so; one significant study found that in Thailand and Indonesia
migration of women between the ages of 15-19 outnumbered
that of males.

Campaigns by women's groups in these countries raise critical questions about the development models their governments have chosen which make them vulnerable to such
exploitation. They are slowly learning to organise into trade
unions to cope with exploitative work conditions in export

processing zones and factories where they are employed as cheap labour to do low- skilled and tedious work in garment or electronics factories. As a young, migrant workforce, they are vulnerable to both economic and sexual exploitation. In the Philippines, for instance, the economic crisis and the ever present threat of retrenchment forces many women to accept sexual harassment on the job. The expression 'Lay down or lay off' has passed into popular parlance, but many are organising to resist such harassment.

It is the militancy, resourcefulness, entrepreneurship and networking skills of impoverished women and men in Asia and other parts of the Third World that the following stories focus on, report and celebrate. Individually, and severally, they are a testimony to their resolve to resist unjust practice and policy through direct action, on the ground, and to compel those in power to recognise that macro-level planning has to synchronise with micro-level living, in order to be viable — and acceptable.

Sujata Madhok

Bhopal women say no to Carbide settlement
Manju Kak and *Sheela Reddy*

New Delhi — For hundreds of thousands of people affected by the disastrous gas leak in Bhopal nearly seven years ago, the 470 million dollar settlement paid by the multinational, Union Carbide, did not close the chapter. Several voluntary organisations representing gas-affected people in Bhopal are challenging the out-of-court settlement between the Indian government and the multinational.

As they anxiously await a verdict from the Supreme Court of India on their petition, several hundred victims, men, women and children, staged a silent sit-in in August 1991 outside the Supreme Court, demanding justice. Their leaders warned that tragedies like theirs could recur because, far from punishing the erring multinational, the government is encouraging wholesale import of potentially hazardous technologies, without laying down safeguards to prevent industrial accidents.

The Bhopal disaster was caused by the leakage of methyl isocyanate (MIC) but the New Industrial Policy lists isocyanates as one of the priority sectors for foreign investment, and the latest budget reduces taxes on isocyanates from 120 per cent to 40 per cent. Victims are also dissatisfied with the compensation offered. They say the settlement was based on arbitrary calculations of the number who died or were injured in the gas leak.

The calculations for compensation, according to the Supreme Court of India, were based on 3,000 dead, 30,000 cases of total or partial disability and 50,000 minor injuries. Activists, who have filed a petition for reviewing the settlement, argue that this is an incredibly low figure, given the 600,000 odd claimants. At the time of the settlement, four years after the tragedy, less than 10 per cent of the claimants had been examined for personal injuries.

"The settlement was arrived at on the basis of medical categorisation that was flawed and unscientific,"claims Indira Jaising of the Lawyer's Collective that provides legal aid to some of the victims. Doctors C.Sathyamala and Nisheeth Vohra, who conducted independent surveys to generate data that would help victims, say the categorisation is supposedly based on a proforma given to patients, but it did not distiguish between disability and injury, as the settlement does. Dr. Sathyamala claims the categorisation is based on a wrong scoring system which is totally against accepted medical practice".

Claims were to be based on medical records. But these were impossible for most victims to produce because government hospitals generally retained the records of outpatients and did not part with them. Nor had the majority of unlettered slum-dwelling victims maintained records, being unaware of such procedures.

Nearly seven years have passed but so far only 3,61,000 have been examined while 2,47,000 still await injury assessment, says Abdul Jabbar Khan, convenor of the largest organisation of victims, the Bhopal Gas Peedit Mahila Udyog Sangathan. A study published by the Indian Council of Medical Research last year indicates that close to 200,000 gas victims continue to suffer from medically diagnosable illneses.

"Health was our greatest asset," mourns Kasturi Bai, a seamstress. Now she is able to work just three days in a month. Her husband, a labourer on daily wages, now works four or five days in a month. Suraiya Bi, mother of eight, nursed her husband, a rickshaw-puller, until he died four years after the gas leak. She herself suffers from mental disorders. Doctors have observed such Post Traumatic Stress Disorder in many gas victims, similar to the mental stress experienced by many prisoners of the Second World War.

But Suraiya Bi is not entitled to medical aid or compensation. Like her, over 90 per cent of those who worked for a living reported a decrease in ability. Some 70-80 per cent are seriously debilitated. "The government has betrayed us," says Zubeida Bi whose husband died three years after the disaster from the after-effects of the deadly gas. "Nearly every month there is a death in someone or the other's home but the doctors say they cannot mention that the dead person was suffering from gas-related complications," says Ameena Bi, whose two grandchildren died six months after the gas leak.

While medical experts say victims of the gas leak suffer from a wide range of respiratory, ocular, behavioural and other disorders, the Indian Council of Medical Research has been unable to prescribe a line of treatment in the absence of clear information about the gas stored in the Bhopal tank.

"In the beginning we used to get fistfuls of tablets at the emergency dispensaries, but now they shoo us away without any medicines," complains 65-year-old Ameena, who suffers from frequent backache and bouts of dizziness and nausea.

Nearly all the women and children say they are frequently ill ever since the disastrous leak. Scores of the women and children who travelled to the capital four years ago on a protest march collapsed on the road and had to be hospitalised. "All our savings went to buy medicines for the family," says Haseena Bi, a mother of two sons, whose husband makes a precarious living as a vegetable vendor. Haseena's husband took a loan of Rs 5000 from the Government to pay for medical treatment for Haseena, who has had spells of headache and nausea ever since she inhaled the deadly gas. "But after we paid all the cuts and commissions, we only got Rs 3500 of the loan," she points out matter-of-factly, adding that her husband works less than 15 days now because of his illness. "Every so often someone wheels him home on his handcart because he suddenly faints on the roadside," she says.

Besides, as Sathyamala's surveys indicate, there is a four-fold increase in spontaneous abortions among the gas-affected women, with the rate of still-births going up as well. "Women's bodies were so affected that many still cannot carry the foetus for the full term. Victims suffer from a disruption in the menstrual cycle, with decreased cycle length and an increased duration of bleeding, she says. As a result, women from the affected areas are now considered less healthy and fertile and men from outside Bhopal are unwilling to marry them. Divorce and separation have become more frequent.

Diagnosis is a problem, since Indian doctors have rarely come across MIC poisoning. The victims cannot pay for expensive private care or buy costly drugs. They are forced to go to overcrowded government-run hospitals. "We stand in long queues for hours, like beggars,"says Sapra Bi, a heart patient who continues to vomit blood. "We have no option." Adds Suraiya Bi,"Without a proper line of treatment, trips to the hospital are in vain."

"We are fighting not just for compensation but for booking the culprits allowed to go scot free," says rubber businessman Ashok Sharma who rescued 18 people on the night of the disaster. Sharma wonders whether the lives he saved by risking his own mean so little. "Is it because the people affected were poor?" he asks. The settlement had been signed by a Congress government; subsequently the National Front government repudiated the dropping of criminal charges. Now, with the Congress back again, the victims are not very hopeful. "This case would have taught multinationals a lesson," says Jabbar Khan, "but now they will continue with the old ways and keep dumping obsolete technology on third world countries".

Several eminent jurists have also denounced the court order on compensation to gas-hit victims as "senseless and cata-strophic". Former Chief Justic of Delhi High Court, Rajinder Sachar, pointed out at a meeting of lawyers: "No one has even cared to take into account the fact that the damage would be genetic, spread across two or three generations." Twenty-six-year-old Saira Banu, the wife of a daily wager, knows this only too well. Her two daughters, born after the gas leak, have been sickly from birth. "When we have the money we buy them medicines, and when we don't, there is nothing we can do about it," says Saira, who had a miscarriage after the accident.

In August 1991, 140 members of parliament signed a petition demanding the setting up of a national commission to review all medical data on gas victims and to ensure treatment and rehabilitation for them. For the survivors of Bhopal, there may still be a slender thread of hope.

Development or disaster?
Rajashri Dasgupta

Calcutta — "My people are afraid of a Bhopal type of industrial disaster. They don't want a fertilizer plant on their doorstep," says Phalguni Choudhury, headman of Gabberia village.

Village folk in the Sunderbans region of the state of West Bengal have staunchly resisted a hundred million rupee fertilizer factory project. Their alertness may have saved the Sunderbans, a deltaic region of mangrove swamps and rare flora and fauna, from ecological destruction. The villagers are convinced that emissions from the fertilizer plant would pollute their environment.

The ghost of the Bhopal gas tragedy of 1984 haunts them, even though Bhopal city is hundreds of miles away. Leakage from the multinational Union Carbide's pesticide plant there killed and poisoned several thousand people in one of the world's worst industrial disasters. Officials of the Sunderbans Fertilizers Ltd (SFL) had proposed to set up a plant at Mandirbazar to produce 66,000 tons of single superphosphate, a cheap and low nutrient fertilizer, and 33,000 tons of sulfuric acid annually. They required 120 bighas (less than an acre) but managed to acquire only 33 bighas.

"Initially many villagers sold their land. They now regret it," says Choudhury. Bishudhananda Pukait adds, "Today no threat or lure of money can coerce the people to sell their land."

Pukait, an unassuming telegraph operator, is the secretary of the Mandirbazar Environment Protection Committee (MEPC), set up to oppose the project.

The MEPC highlighted the dangers of chemical pollution. A village science club emerged which held many small workshops on issues like the Bhopal disaster and the atomic threat. Local boys composed limericks and staged street plays. Folk songs and dances were adapted to highlight the consequences of industrial pollutants. Posters and pamphlets urged villagers not to sell their land. The awareness and enthusiasm generated by this peaceful cultural movement was amazing.

Jharna Sardar, community health guide and mother of three, reacts angrily when the project is mentioned. "It is the women and children who will suffer most if harmful gases are emitted by the plant. In Bhopal it is the women who have borne the burden of nursing the sick and bringing up crippled children," she says. Gostho Baidya was offered an exorbitant Rs 80,000 for eight bighas of land whose market value is Rs 20,000. He still refused to sell to the company. The villagers were pressured by the District Commissioner and the member of the legislature from the area but to no avail.

The promoter of SFL, Dilip Roy Chowdhury, formerly sheriff of Calcutta city and a top official of the firm Reckitt and Coleman, initially dismissed the agitation as a "minor irritant", led by "motivated and misguided people" and encouraged by a "hostile press". However, the company has now been forced to withdraw the move to set up the plant in Mandirbazar. They are looking for another site. This will be third time the plant site has been shifted because of resistance by villagers.

Fertilizer plants are listed among the 20 hazardous industries by the central government. In 1985 the project was rejected by the then Central Minister for Chemicals and Fertilizers, Veerendra Patil. But in February 1986 a high-powered committee approved it. West Bengal's Pollution Control Board then approved it, even though the Sunderbans had been declared a biosphere reserve. The Member Secretary of the Board, B.R. Sengupta, later reportedly admitted that the Board had been under pressure to clear the project.

The two existing phosphate plants in the state, in Rishra and Kharda, are infamous for the environmental hazards they cause. They are among the 25 factories declared dangerous by the government after the Bhopal disaster. "Such harmful units should be located far from heavily populated areas," says Pukait. Waving aside these fears, local political leaders say the factory would have provided employment to at least 1000 people. In a monocrop area, where people find wage labour for only two to three months in the year and search for work in neighbouring Calcutta the rest of the time, this employment would have been a boon, they argue.

SFL officials had publicly said they would spend ten million rupees on pollution control measures, but the people were not satisfied. "During the monsoons this entire low lying region is flooded. Factory effluents will definitely spill over to adjacent agricultural areas," says Dilip Baidhya, the local schoolteacher who has composed numerous popular rhymes attacking the project. The fact that the plant was to be located within a mile of the only water well was cited as another concern. "As it is there is water scarcity. The plant would consume a lot of water and lower the water level," fears Jharna Sardar.

But the most crucial factor is that Mandirbazar, known as the 'Gateway of the Sunderbans', is just 5 kms from the embankments of this coastal region. As Sikha Mondal, a student, put it, "A streamlet acts as sewer for this area and it ends in the Sunderbans waters. Can you imagine the disaster for the fragile ecosystem of the Sunderbans if the streamlet is flooded with effluents from the factory?"

Another possible danger was that toxic substances in the streams could wipe out marine life in the Sunderbans, throwing hundreds of fisherfolk out of employment. The debate over the project still continues in Mandirbazar and elsewhere. Worldwide, the choice between industrialization and environmental destruction is a highly controversial one. But one thing is clear: increasingly, India's villagers are unwilling to pay the price of industrial development strategies which benefit elite groups but leave them worse off than before.

Tendu leaf politics
Ilina Sen

Raipur — The tender leaves of the tendu tree caused much political intrigue and infighting in the recent elections in the central Indian state of Madhya Pradesh. Dried and rolled up, the tendu leaves make bidis — the poor person's cigarettes. Bidis are big business in India and the bidi contractors and manufacturers' lobby is a powerful one.

Last year political exigency caused the then Chief Minister of the province to challenge the monopoly of the contractors who corner the leaf cheap and sell it dear. He ordered that the government buy the leaf directly from the forest people who pick it.

Traditionally, tendu leaf pickers are forest dwelling tribals. Women, men and children harvest the leaves seasonally, picking them and bundling them. They are paid subsistence wages by the contractors who buy collection rights from the forest department. The forest districts of Madhya Pradesh and adjoining Maharashtra state grow 75 per cent of the country's tendu leaf.

The Chief Minister's move to set up co-operative societies of the leaf pickers was calculated to win him local support and votes. The strategy did not quite pay off because infighting in the party led to his ouster and the subsequent Congress government delayed payments to the cooperatives, leaving the operation in the doldrums. The party could not use the co-operatives to win the election.

Half-hearted though the co-operative effort has been, it is still a great advance for pickers like Theresa Tirkey. For 10 years Tirkey and her colleagues have struggled for fair wages. Social activists began organising these workers in the early eighties, demanding an end to the contract system, sale of leaf directly to the government, payment of government stipulated minimum wages, and equal wages for women. In Raigarh and Bastar in Madhya Pradesh and in Chandrapur and Gadhchiroli in Maharashtra, there were strikes amd militant action every year from 1985 onwards.

In 1982-83, the government minimum wage for labourers was Rs.5 (US 27 cents) per day. However, in tendu picking, men earned Rs. 2, women got Rs. 1.50 and children Rs. 1. Under pressure wages rose slowly, going upto Rs. 11 in 1988. But workers and their leaders paid a heavy price.

Tirkey will never forget the night of May 8, 1986. A demonstration had been planned by her organisation, the Joshpur Samaj Sewa Samiti, for the following morning. But that night the police picked her up from her home in Tangarpani. "I was tortured, even though I was two months' pregnant. I suffered a miscarriage and was barely able to stand when I was released from custody three weeks later," she recalls. The case she subsequently filed against the police is still dragging on in the court. Yet, the agitation achieved a major victory — it established the principle of equal wages for men and women in the whole of Raigarh district.

Last year, local people elected Tirkey head of the Panchayat (the local decision-making body) in an open contest, defeating five male contenders. It was a rare honour for a woman in rural India. During the 1989 season (mid-April to June) Theresa Tirkey and her group of women maintained a strict vigil over collection and payment for the tendu leaf they picked through a co-operative set up by the government. Each of them earned Rs. 15 for every bundle of 100 leaves, compared to the Rs. 11 they had got before. They were also entitled to a share of the profits earned after the leaf was auctioned to bidi manufacturers.

The sudden introduction of cooperatives was a coup of sorts. The government marshalled the entire revenue department and teachers from government schools to supervise the operation. Primary cooperative societies were formed under the minor forest produce collection corporation. The corporation's Chairman claimed, "The government's action is a unique achievement, a step in the direction of making the primary collectors the owners of forest wealth."

Opposition to the move came not just from the wealthy

contractors but also from an unexpected source — the ultra-left Naxalite groups operating under cover in the forests. They felt the move was meant to take the edge off the people's struggle they are leading.

The auctions netted the government a bonanza of Rs.2.07 billion (US$ 121 million). The Bharatiya Janata Party's (BJP) government, which came to power is reluctant to distribute this money to the cooperatives. The BJP cannot afford to alienate the tribals, but it is under pressure from the contractors. Caught between conflicting interests the BJP government has, on the one hand, increased wages for the picking season from Rs. 15 to Rs. 25, but on the other hand, has let the contractors re-enter the business. While cooperatives will continue to collect the leaf and sell it to the government the contractors will buy the green leaf from the government and sell it to the manufacturers after drying it.

The cooperativisation policy was criticised on many accounts. There were allegations that the corporation had sold the leaf to the favoured buyers at low prices, that the trees were not pruned, causing lower yields, that leaf collection was lower, leading to unemployment among bidi makers. All these factors allegedly combined to push up the price of bidis by over one rupee per packet. The government is using the plea that the cooperativisation caused prices to rise, to bring back the contractors.

The Congress party, now in the opposition, threatens to begin an agitation against the changed policy and is demanding immediate distribution of the dividend to the cooperatives. The Chief Minister has held meetings at which the dividend is symbolically distributed to the pickers.

Women like Hora from Kunkuri welcomed the wage hike and want dividends but feel the tendu policy should be holistic. "We must have free access to government-owned forests and take care of the trees, only then will they bear leaf and fruit for our sustenance," she says.

A SPARC of hope for slum-dwellers
Deepa Gahlot

Bombay — "We are no longer afraid of the police," says Rehmat Sheikh confidently. "Even if there is a fight in the slum at two in the night, we women go to the police station to sort it out." Sheikh lives in a slum in India's west coast metropolis, Bombay. She is a member of Mahila Milan, a women's organisation that has given its members a new militancy. "Nobody listened to us when we were alone but now we're organised and strong," adds Laxmi Naidu, another member. "Singly, we were thin sticks which could be easily broken. Together, we are like a thick bundle. Unbreakable."

Mahila Milan was formed by SPARC (Society for the Promotion of Area Resource Centres) four years ago, to empower slum women and make them self-reliant. Most women in the 'E Ward' slum, where Mahila Milan began work, were unlettered migrants from rural areas They were unable to tackle day-to-day problems like admitting a sick child to hospital or talking to the municipal authorities. SPARC workers taught them how to deal with authority figures and fill up forms for ration cards (which provide access to subsidised foodgrain), bank loans and electricity connections. Mahila Milan members met the inspectors of neighbourhood police posts and told them that if there was any trouble in the area, members would deal with it. SPARC director Sheela Patel says, "Earlier when one of these women saw a policeman, her hand went to her pocket to see how much she had to bribe him. Now, when she goes to a police station she is offered a cup of tea."

The respect accorded to Mahila Milan members comes from a recognition of the solid community work they are doing. The E Ward office of Mahila Milan is run by local women like Rehmat Sheikh, Leela Naidu, Sona Pujari and Shehnaaz Sheikh, who previously did domestic work and fetched milk or dropped children to school for a small fee. Seated in their untidy little office, housed in a municipal dispensary building, the women exude confidence. They recall how, when some families were refused ration cards, they led a group of 40 women to the ration office and convinced officials to give them cards. Families living in pavement shacks initially got temporary and later permanent cards.

Apart from entitling a family to cheaper food, ration cards establish identity and place of residence. The latter is critical for those squatting on government land, in the hope of getting legal ownership of a small plot. Housing is the biggest problem of E Ward families. The area has the largest number of pavement colonies in the city, and demolition by municipal authorities is a major and ever-present threat.

Mahila Milan encourages saving for housing and other needs. Naidu and Shehnaz Sheikh collect small savings from the members every month and deposit them in a common housing fund. "No matter how small the amount is, over a period of time the collective savings add up. In four years we have saved Rs 4,50,000 (US$ 25,000) for housing," says Naidu.

Besides this, the women have also put together Rs 40,000 (US$ 2222) for daily emergencies. Whenever a member needs money for medicine, goods to sell, children's schoolbooks or clothes, the loan is made from this account at a nominal interest rate of two rupees a month. The housing fund is not touched. The loan scheme is useful since, according to SPARC surveys, 74 per cent of slum-dwellers earn less than the minimum daily wage of Rs 18 (US$ 1). Women make up 27 per cent of the work-force and 90.9 per cent of them earn less than the minimum wage.

In some areas Mahila Milan, with SPARC help, has initiated income generation projects for women, teaching them to stitch, make files, folders and decorative items. Adult education classes are also offered. Mahila Milan branches have been set up in the Dharavi, Wadala, Goregaon, Mankhurd and Chembur areas of Bombay; branches have also sprung up in two south Indian cities, Madras and Bangalore.

The collective strength of Mahila Milan's 500 members in E Ward was demonstrated when they courageously took the Bombay Municipal Corporation (BMC) to court. BMC staff frequently destroy unauthorised pavement huts and take away the pavement dwellers' belongings, selling or destroying them. In 1989 the women won their case against BMC and got compensation for goods illegally snatched during demolition. Trained by SPARC, the women had noted down the number of the BMC van which took their belongings away. They also made a detailed list of goods taken from each hut, down to the smallest spoon, and brought in a photographer to take pictures as evidence.

The eviction issue has been central to the work of SPARC and other progressive organisations. In 1981, when the BMC decided that pavement huts were illegal and started its demolition and eviction drives, civil liberties groups took the matter to court. Initially, they were able to secure a stay on demolitions, but in July 1985 the Supreme Court withdrew the stay order and gave the state the right to demolish. It was at this time that a group of people decided to form SPARC, recognising the need to organise slum and pavement dwellers and help them fight for their rights.

SPARC did not wish to be a charity organisation. They first created an information base, collecting data on the pavement and slum dwellers and charting out their requirements; they then helped the people to organise to obtain those needs. They focussed on women slum and pavement dwellers, since many government and voluntary agency programmes ignore them.

"We thought we would start with the worst situation. Things could only get better here," says Director Patel. "Most of us had worked with other institutions in the area and found the welfare approach didn't work. The government welfare agencies were wary of taking up the issue of pavement dwellers, and nobody believed we could organise slum dwellers on such a large scale." The SPARC team covered 6,000 households and nearly 27,000 individuals, in their survey asking questions about background, income, family structure, etc., that no one had bothered to find out before. Says Mithu Gupta, a SPARC coordinator, "People have the idea that pavement dwellers are a strain on civic resources, when the truth is, they pay for water and toilet facilities; but whenever resettlement plans are made the houses are designed according to middle class perceptions of living. And resettlement in distant places usually deprives slum-dwellers of their jobs."

SPARC and Mahila Milan work in conjunction with the National Slum Dwellers' Federation (NSDF), a complementary body that helps in research, negotiation and other activities. NSDF leader A. Jockin says, "Planners decide arbitrarily what is good for the poor, based on global patterns. But macro-level planning should synchronise with micro-level living." The objective is to help slum-dwellers participate in decisions regarding policy and implementation when it affects them. Explains Jockin, "SPARC and NSDF cooperate to form people's groups. They have certain limitations. so we take over. "For example, we participated in meetings related to a World Bank project for housing the economically weaker sections. Our coordination with SPARC enabled them to help 10,000 people apply for the scheme. On their own, local people wouldn't have known how to complete the formalities."

Collaboration has given NSDF certain new perspectives. "Till now organisations like ours were male-dominated. We only used women for demonstrations. Now we want them to take leadership roles, and this has happened as a result of the relationship with SPARC," Jockin admits.

Housing design is an important part of their work. Middle class people are used to a toilet in each home, but for a large slum family living in a single room, a public toilet is more suitable. Similarly, squatters are unused to multi-storey living. Since the women usually do piece-work at home, they need a front or back yard for it or, alternatively, a workshop in the vicinity.

SPARC's practical approach is evident in the Markandeya Society housing scheme coming up in Dharavi, Asia's largest slum. Chelliah Shankaralingam says it took a three-year struggle to get loans and subsidies and change the housing pattern to suit the members' requirements. "Dharavi residents who subscribed to government-aided schemes found prices escalating and the design unsuitable. They sold off incomplete houses. But Markandeya Society people managed to make the authorities see their point of view. In a few months their affordable, model houses will be ready," says Shankaralingam.

In 1988 when the Indian Railways decided to clear huts within 50 ft. of suburban tracks, thousands risked displacement. The question of resettlement came up, but first a proper census of these dwellers was required. SPARC was assigned the survey. It shared the census results with the communities settled along the tracks and a Railway Slum Dwellers' Federation was formed to represent them. Members were trained to study resettlement strategies and negotiate with the authorities. One heartening result is that a slum colony along the Mankhurd track is being resettled close by. Construction has begun, despite the hostility of some government officials who feel "these people are being pampered".

SPARC has spread its work to distant areas like Dindoshi. In 1986 hundreds of huts were demolished and families dumped on a piece of land here with no water, electricity, toilets, roads or street lights. Over the years welfare organisations helped people build homes. The BMC eventually provided lighting, taps and toilets, but it treated the people as squatters living in illegal dwellings. BMC now claims this is a model township. But most women here are unemployed, having lost their jobs as domestics in localities near their old homes. The men find commuting a strain, and about a third of the people have returned to their old areas.

It took SPARC five years to get a piece of land in Dindoshi, to construct permanent, legal housing. A cooperative society has been set up here by the local Mahila Milan branch, and fifty houses, a community hall, a park and public toilets are being built on the 18,000 sq. ft. plot. Says Lopez Isaac, a SPARC worker, "The houses will have high ceilings to enable the building of a mezzanine floor. This is the pattern of slum housing in Bombay and it ensures optimum utilisation of space. We had to fight for the increased height, but we got it." He adds. "Our strategy was not to give anything. People have to demand their rights. Other welfare agencies gave dole and some people built houses. But we managed to get our members the security of legal possession of authorised houses."

SPARC has also conducted an eight-city study of brown sugar addiction for the government's social work department and a study of street and other vulnerable urban children; they hope to work with them in the future.

Patel says government and municipal authorities are grudgingly but increasingly supportive. "That's because SPARC activists are not stereotypes of what activists should be like. We cut out all activist language. The whole idea is to get equal on the negotiation table, create relationships, argue extensively but never close doors. We see our role as one of educating both sides. The officials are learning to negotiate with the poor and vice versa."

The organisation's aim now, says Gupta, is to work in other cities to ensure that Bombay's mistakes are not repeated. One of their publications summarises it well : "As more people migrate from the villages, there must be some channel through which the past experience of the urban poor can help those who flee to the cities."

Resisting the industrial invasion
Shree Venkatram

Bangalore — Scientists have invaded the heart of a virgin rain forest, on the banks of a green river, to build a nuclear power plant in the south Indian state of Karnataka. The Kaiga nuclear plant is not the only instance of the industrial invasion of Karnataka's Western Ghats region. In Kusnur the government has also handed over 70,000 acres of village common lands to a company to grow eucalyptus trees to meet the raw material needs of a private mill.

Neither move has gone unchallenged in a state whose people are among the most environmentally aware in India today. Local agitations have sprung up to protest against these projects, backed by the expertise of environment groups in Karnataka and neighbouring states. In Sirsi town, near the Kaiga plant site, a relay hunger strike has been going on for months outside a state government office. Literacy levels are high here and pro-environment ideas have spread fast.

Says Kripa, a woman activist of Citizens for Alternatives to Nuclear Energy (CANE), "The farmers are well informed about the hazards the nuclear plant will pose. They are educated and read local newspapers and tabloids which are highlighting the issue. We at CANE feed these small papers with the latest information on the nuclear front. Our supporters also distribute pamphlets."

Last October, hundreds converged at the Kaiga project office at Karwar, demanding that work on the plant be abandoned. More than 300 people, including many women and the religious leader, Swami Vishweshar Teertha of Pejawar, courted arrest. Signature and newspaper campaigns, rallies and hunger strikes in the district and anti-nuclear marches and road shows in the state capital, Bangalore, have been the methods of protest adopted. The people question the wisdom of locating a nuclear plant in a remote forest, especially since it has high rainfall and wind velocity. Kripa points out, "During the monsoon rains, Kaiga is inaccessible. The government suspends even the normal bus service. But it expects to be able to evacuate the whole township in a matter of minutes should an emergency arise. Moreover, Kaiga is near seven dams and in a tectonically weak zone."

The unexpected resistance to the Kaiga plant is the result of environment consciousness created in Karnataka over recent years by dedicated activist groups. These groups are alarmed at the denudation of the 1600-km long Western Ghats, a mountain range which runs along India's western coast, bordering the Arabian Sea. One morning, six years ago, a small but determined group marched from Sakalani village to a forest area 12 kms away where a contractor's men were felling trees. The 30-odd men and women, many with babes in their arms, rushed forward, each hugging a tree. The contractor's men ran away.

Inspiration for that non-violent attempt to save their trees had come from Sunderlal Bahuguna, a leader of the Chipko movement (the world famous ecology movement in north

India's Himalayan belt). He had visited nearby Sirsi town and addressed a gathering a few days earlier. He had told them about how villagers had clung to trees to save them from the axe. The people realised they too could prevent destruction of the forests; they knew only too well that because the forests had been ravaged women had to trek twice the distance to collect fuelwood and fodder. Herbs for treatment of ailments were becoming difficult to find, and water had actually become scarce in an area that received over 3000 mm of rainfall a year.

The Kurbas, the traditional honey-gatherers, and the Medars, who fashioned items from bamboo and cane, had been driven to starvation, for the trees which sustained them had been grabbed by greedy outsiders. Timber contractors, rayon and paper mill owners had bought up whole forests to meet industrial and urban needs. Bamboo and softwood factories had denuded the mountains and polluted the rivers — the Cauvery, the Kapila and the Tungabhadra, to mention a few. Cattle which drank polluted water produced premature calves, fish died and people got skin allergies.

Further, the government's social forestry schemes only benefitted the rich. Eucalyptus was planted to meet the raw material requirements of the mills, it produced little fuelwood and did not allow undergrowth to grow for cattle to feed on.

Nagesh Hedge, a journalist who has long observed the environmental movement says, "Even before the Saklani march, farmers had opposed eucalyptus by pulling out the saplings. Then in 1980, the Totgarh Farmers' Cooperative had stalled the Bethi Dam which would have submerged thousands of fertile acres under water. The Saklani march, however, set the trend for villagers to gather at felling sites and protest by hugging the trees." The local press termed the protest Appiko' which means 'embrace' in Kannada. The Appiko movement spread, forest officers were picketed and the government forced to ban clear felling in the state.

In 1987 voluntary groups working with villagers in Karnataka and three adjoining states joined to organise the 'Save the Western Ghats' march. Two groups marched from the two ends of the Ghats, spreading the message of conservation and learning first-hand the extent of deforestation and pollution. The marchers included several scientists.

Today village women in Kusnur are in the forefront of the environment struggle, demanding that the 70,000 acres leased out for eucalyptus be returned to the people. Most villagers, being landless, depend on village commons for grazing cattle and gathering firewood and fruit from the trees. People have uprooted eucalyptus and replaced it with shady, fruit-bearing trees.

The Samaj Parivartana Samudaya, a voluntary group leading the protest has filed a public interest case against the leasing of the land, and the Supreme Court has stayed its transfer till the case is heard.

Women miners refuse retrenchment
Ilina Sen

Raipur—"We work much harder than these management men. Retrench them, not us," says Ghashinbai contemptuously.

For ten years now Ghashinbai and other women miners of Chattisgarh in central India have resisted all efforts to throw them out of their jobs. These women break iron ore in the captive mines of the Bhilai steel plant in Dalli Rajhara, Mahamaya, Aridongri and Kokan. The mines are owned by the steel plant and worked by a combination of manual and mechanized processes. Women work only in the manual mines; there is not a single woman among the skilled workers in the mechanized mines of the steel plant. Also, no women work underground since the law forbids them to do this "hazardous" work. The ore is blasted by male workers and subsequently gangs of men and women break it into specified sizes. Payment is by piece rate, according to different sizes and grades of ore. Men and women are paid equal rates.

Some years ago, the Steel Authority of India, which runs the Bhilai steel plant and other units, embarked on a policy of complete mechanization of the mines. To do this, it needed to retrench the manual workers. As a first step, it launched a selective attack on the women workers. The impact of this policy is evident in the Hirri dolomite mines near Bilaspur, which is also a captive mine of the Bhilai steel plant. The management floated a "voluntary retirement" scheme for women with over 20 years of service left, luring them with attractive cash incentives. At the same time, their husbands were offered regular employment at the main plant, 150 kms away. Women who refused, faced the prospect of breaking up the family unit.

This carrot and stick approach has eased 200 women out of work since 1987, in a region where thousands are unemployed and job opportunities severely limited. A similar trend is evident in the mining industry as a whole. The female workforce shrank from over 20 per cent in 1951 to less than 12 per cent in 1971. In coal mining the decline was even more dramatic — from 15 per cent in 1957 to 5 per cent in 1971. In the wake of the nationalization of the coal mines in 1972-73, over 50,000 women lost their jobs. In the iron ore mines, women's share fell from 28 per cent to 22 per cent between 1962 and 1976. Today, 2130 women work in the Bhilai mines compared to 3443 men.

When coal was nationalized, the unions quietly accepted retrenchment of female workers. But, today, unions like Chattisgarh Mines Shramik Sangh (CMSS) are committed to the cause of their female membership. CMSS began organizing iron workers in 1977. The workers were mostly employed through contractors and paid a pittance. No facilities were provided. Women had no maternity benefits or security and were subject to sexual harassment by contractors and supervisors.

Women participated in CMSS activity in large numbers. Unlettered first generation workers like Kusumbai and Anusuyabai became leaders. Kusum died during childbirth in 1977 and Anusuya was killed when police fired on agitating workers. Today Durgabai carries their mantle. The union has educated its women workers on the threat of mechanization and "voluntary retirement" schemes. It demands a rational approach to modernization, keeping the workers' interests in mind. A strong argument against selective retrenchment of women is that their attendance and work performance is as good as that of the men, sometimes better. For instance, in the Jharandalli cooperative in 1986-87, women worked 632 hours while men worked 365.

In 1988, the women of the Dalli-Rajhara mines organized a seminar on the issue of mechanization, female labour and retrenchment at Hirri, with the support of several trade unions. They demanded scrapping of the voluntary retirement scheme, a halt to mechanization until the unemployment problem is resolved, transfer of both husband and wife to the same place and not separately, recruitment of only women to jobs vacated by women as well as training and upgradation of the skills of the women workers.

These demands are still to be met. But the women are not giving up. They are alert, expecting further attacks on their right to work. Says CMSS organizer Durgabai, "Not a single woman in my mine has given up her job. But the threat of retrenchment still hangs over our heads."

Troubles in tribal country
Maitreyi Chatterjee

Galudi — The quiet towns of Galudi and Ghatsila used to be havens. The pleasant climate of these places, located in the southern part of Bihar, attracted people wanting a peaceful holiday. The river Subarnarekha flowed gently past Galudi, separating it from the tribal villages and the distant hills which shelter elephants. Winters here were particularly pleasant, the sunshine mellow and the air crisp.

All that changed when the Subarnarekha Multipurpose Project (SMP) was conceived in 1974. This $127 million World Bank financed project has transformed the face of Galudi, Chandil and other small towns. Two major dams, two barrages and seven canals are being constructed on the Subarnarekha and its tributaries. The project's objective, according to the Bihar state government, is to provide irrigation to 255,000 hectares of land in Bihar and the neighbouring states of Orissa and West Bengal. In addition it is supposed to provide water for industrial and municipal use in the Singbhum district and to reduce flood damage in Orissa and West Bengal.

Brisk work is now on at the Galudi barrage. Materials are pouring in from all over the district. The huge quantity of stone chips needed is being locally procured from the hillocks of solid rock which abound in the region. The peace of the tribal areas has been shattered by the constant blasting of hillocks, night and day. Innumerable trucks roar through the region, carrying dynamited rocks to the barrage sites. Contractors employ hundreds of female labourers at several sites to break the rocks into chips.

Savitri, Radhamoni and Bharati of Uldah village, Somvari of Kumarmuri and Guruvari of Deoli are a few of the tribals employed by the contractors. They are young women, in their teens and early twenties. They belong to the Ho, Munda and Bhumij tribes. "The contractor knew a man in my village and sent him word that women were needed for crushing stones. Since the wages were higher than those at home, I accepted," explains Somvari. Agriculture cannot provide us work through-out the year,' adds Anjana, another worker.

Though the SMP is a government project, workers are employed through private contractors. Employing contract labour enables government departments to evade labour laws on paying minimum wages and providing welfare benefits. The contractors pay extremely low wages for long hours of work that is seasonal or sporadic.

"We get up at four in the morning so that we can reach the collection points on time for the truck that takes us to the site," says Savitri, stifling a yawn. "We work from eight o'clock to one o'clock, take a short break and resume work. We get dropped at the collection point late in the evening and from there we walk home."

The work involves breaking blocks of stone into chips and carrying them to the trucks. Wages depend on output but wage calculations are arbitrary. Carrying loads over a distance of 100 ft fetches Rs 3-5; wages for a fortnight amount to Rs 160.

"Our income depends on the whims of the truckers," complains Radhamoni. "Often, after we have finished crushing the stones there is not a truck in sight. We cannot load. This means Rs 50-60 less per month. And when trucks break down we remain out of work till they are repaired." Further, the women must pay four days' wages each month as commission to the contractors, for providing them employment.

Flying chips frequently cause injuries to the women. But they are provided no safety gear such as helmets or masks. What happens if someone is injured? "Nothing." says Bharti. "We get no money for treatment. In fact we lose money if we are unable to report for duty."

There are other hazards too. The women work in a cloud of dust which over a period causes congestion of the lungs. The constant bending leads to backaches and gynaecological problems. Ear splitting noise levels affect their hearing. Yet there are no medical facilities on the sites. "Forget about doctors, we don't even have drinking water," complains Bharati.

Worse, rumours of sexual harassment are rife. Asked if this is true, the women look hestiantly at each other. Anjana, the most articulate, says, "So far we have not faced it. But it would be untruthful to say it does not exist." A political activist, Gita Das, is blunt. "Many women workers are forced to live with contractors, site engineers and officials. They are constantly replaced by newer, younger women. Poverty prevents them from refusing."

Tribal women are looked upon as easy game, since they come from communities that are being increasingly pauperised. Tribals such as the Ho, Santhal, Munda, Gond and Oraon, among others, are the original inhabitants of Singbhum. But increasingly the district has been invaded by outsiders. The influx has been rapid because Singbhum abounds in mineral wealth. It has one of the richest iron ore belts in the world besides deposits of minerals like copper, manganese, uranium, chromite and many others.

In 1931 tribals constituted 54 per cent of the population, but by 1981 it had fallen to 44. Over this period the number of towns grew from four to 24. The urban population is overwhelmingly non-tribal, and it is these people who grab the skilled and semi-skilled jobs in the quarries, factories, mines, irrigation, power and construction projects. The tribals, who lack schooling, provide cheap unskilled labour.

"Even our brothers don't attend school. Where is the money?" says Guruvari, as she hammers at a rock. Her family's land is mortgaged to a non-tribal moneylender and her wages largely go towards paying uxurious interest rates. Her father is a sharecropper on someone else's fields. Agricultural yields here are poor—only 3.5 Per cent of the land is irrigated. And the government's establishment of a state monopoly on forest products has deprived the people of a major source of income and sustenance. Hundreds of acres have been appropriated by the state and private contractors for mining minerals. Each new project requires import of skilled labour and the building of colonies to house their families. The new towns have swallowed up acres of land.

Ironically, the barrage the tribal women are helping to build at Galudi will only complete the ruination of their families. Several thousand acres of tribal land will be submerged by the Subarnarekha project. Instead of irrigation the SMP will actually provide water for use by the growing industries and mushrooming towns.

But the Guruvaris and Somvaris have no choice. They dare not think beyond the present.

Women's long march for fuel and fodder
Sheela Reddy

New Delhi — "Probably no other group is more affected by environmental degradation than poor village women," says Anil Agarwal of the Centre for Science and Environment, the only organisation in India to have brought out several comprehensive reports on the state of India's environment and its impact on its 800 million people.

Agarwal points out that environmental degradation, brought about by industrialisation, urbanisation and the penetration of cash economy has stretched the already heavy work load of rural women to unbearable limits. As forests continue to be cut down by timber contractors and miners, village women are forced to trek further in search of scarce fuel, fodder and drinking water for their families. Studies show that women spend an incredible average of 7.2 hours a day in fetching fuel and water for the family.

Pointing out that the destruction of natural resources brings about extremely harsh and immediate problems for rural women, dependent entirely on their immediate environment for their family's survival, Agarwal says that few voluntary organisations or even the Indian government have given much though to the increasing problems faced by women in collecting fuel, fodder and water.

Srilata Batliwala, a nutritionist working in the slums of Bombay, agrees: "Startling figures about the rate of deforestation are bandied about. But the real human face of this crisis is the face of women."

Agarwal says the increasing workload on women caused by environmental degradation has several implications: because there is little fuel available for cooking, rural families are faced with grave risks of infection and illness from eating stale or undercooked food; while women are getting more malnourished their increasing household chores leave them with little time for seeking medical care; and women are forced to have more children in order to cope with their inhuman workload.

As Batliwala points out, "Children have become the unwitting victims of the continuing energy hunger in third world villages . . . A family below the poverty line, which does not have the means either to hire labour or purchase labour-saving devices, is compelled to meet its energy needs only by producing several children." This, says Agarwal, has important implications not only for the education, health and nutrition of children but also for the country's massive family planning programmes and the health of women. "If underfed and overworked women are expected to bear many children, the impact on their health will obviously be drastic," he adds.

Moreover, the growth of the cash economy is drawing men away from their villages, leaving women to cope with all the farming work, besides their other onerous chores. The result, predicts Agarwal, is disaster "both for the environment and for the people in these villages, especially the women". As firewood grows scarce, increasing amounts of dung — traditionally used as manure — will be burned as fuel, and because of the lack of manure the productivity of the land will decline further.

However, growing awarness of energy and environment problems has led the government to promote new technologies like biogas plants, fuelwood plantations, smokeless stoves, latrines and handpumps. But most of these programmes have been a dismal failure. This is because women were seldom involved either when the technology was being developed or when it was being disseminated, explains Agarwal.

For instance, when a community biogas plant was set up in a village in the northern state of Uttar Pradesh, the plant came to a grinding halt in less than a year. Agarwal says the village women were very critical of the plant because it was decided, without consulting them, that gas supply would be limited to two hours in the morning, when they were out working in the fields. The women also complained that the gas did not even provide 25 per cent of their fuel needs, forcing them to go in search of wood, instead of the dung cakes they normally used. Further, the new technology increased their dependence on men, even for routine cleaning of the burners.

But where women have been involved in environmental projects, the success rate has been very high. The famous Chipko movement, where hill women hugged trees to prevent contractors from felling them, is typical of women's keen interest in preserving their environment. Since its birth over a decade ago, Chipko has grown into a women-based movement for community tree-planting and a kind of watch-dog village committee against illegal felling of trees, and has spread to other regions of the country as well.

Chandi Prasad Bhatt, a Chipko leader, recalls how a land-

slide brought home to villagers the importance of tree-planting. His organisation, the Dasohli Gram Swaraj Mandal
(DGSM) now organises regular eco-development camps for
villagers in the Himalayan region.

The DGSM workers first find out the villagers' list of priorities
before imposing their own, and help them with it. In one
village, for instance, the women insisted that their biggest
problem was not fuel and fodder but protection from wild
animals. DGSM workers then suggested building a wall around
the fields and planting trees only in the protected space
between the walls and fields. Soon villagers were harvesting
headloads of grass from the protected area.

Movements like Chipko are signs of a growing militancy
amongst poor women to protect and enrich the natural
resources that sustain them, according to Agarwal. "But before
these straws in the wind can come together to form a powerful
movement for change, there is still a long way to go."

PAKISTAN

Women emerge in strength
Imrana Khwaja

Lahore — Zuleikha Begum and the women of her household
sit on a reed mat outside their home chatting with their guests,
while one of the men of the family brings cups of hot, sweet
tea for the visitors. In the macho environment of a Pakistani
village this is an amazing sight.

Getting the men to pour out the tea is not the only change
effected by a unique mass organisation in Pakistan's southern
province of Sindh. The Sindhiani Tehrik (literally Sindhi
Women's Movement), has brought several changes in the lives
of people like Zuleikha Begum. "My grandfather was a hari
(peasant), my father was a hari, and my husband is a hari. We
have no money, and I have had no education. But the
Sindhiani Tehrik has given me awareness," says Zuleikha

Begum. She and her husband eke out a living for themselves and their six children from a mere three acres of land in Sindh's Thatta district.

Sindh is a harsh land, both in its terrain and its feudal structure which perpetuates oppressive customs. Patriarchy is so entrenched here that most non-governmental organisations would find it difficult to work here. But the Tehrik has made significant inroads. While urban women's organisations are satisfied if they can bring 250 women out on the streets on any issue, during the Movement for Restoration of Democracy in 1983, Sindhiani rallied an astounding 25,000 women for a protest in Hyderabad city. "Our membership is spread throughout the districts of Sindh," says Mariam Palejo, a founder member. "While our total membership is about 20,000, there are 5,000 active members." Being an active member doesn't just mean doing work in one's spare time. It means Sindhiani work gets priority. Even the family has to take a back seat."

Sindhiani Tehrik was set up in 1983 as the women's wing of the Awami Tehrik political party. Previously, party women had tried to organise and provide support to wives of male political workers jailed during successive agitations. The fact that Sindhiani Tehrik began by concentrating on the isssues of class and Sindhi nationalism helped it to gain acceptance in the province. Explains Palejo, "The class issue gained us the support of the majority of men and the nationality question made us acceptable to some landlords." The organisation's ability to neutralise, to a great extent, resistance from Sindhi men has been its most astonishing achievement. The freedom with which Sindhiani women carry out their work would be surprising in Pakistani cities, let alone rural areas. "I spend 20 out of 30 days of the month touring around Sindh," says Zahida Sheikh, a member of the central committee. Sheikh is from a conservative lower middle class family of the small town of Kamber, and faced stiff family resistance when she joined the movement. "My parents would not allow me to work for Sindhiani. I went through a long period of depression and spent days lying in bed, with a sheet over my face. Finally they permitted me to take up a job with the social welfare department. Once I was not dependent on them for bus fares and other expenses they could no longer stop me from working for Sindhiani. Now I have given up the job and work full-time for the organisation." Although she makes light of her struggle, it has cost her a great deal. "Only one of my sisters is at all sympathetic towards me. I am alienated from my parents and four other sisters and brothers; they treat me like a stranger," says she.

But Sheikh and Palejo are welcomed in the homes of Sindhiani women throughout the province as though they were family. While it still retains links with the Awami Tehrik party, Sindhiani Tehrik has been autonomous for the last two years. Palejo explains the way they work: "When we first go to a village we start by talking to women about their problems. At first they do not seem conscious of their troubles." But when the worker asks about their personal lives, their relationships with their husbands, their health, education and so on, the women begin to articulate their problems and to understand their lives a little.

"Our help extends beyond talk to practical assistance," she adds, pointing out that Sindhiani has intervened in many cases where child marriages were about to take place, and even forced maulvis (priests) to declare such marriages illegal. Besides, the organisation has handled problems with the police and staged successful sit-ins to demand schools and health centres.

For instance, if a woman's husband beats her, Sindhiani members first try to talk it out with the couple. They also ask other men to talk to the husband or try to settle the marital dispute with the help of elders of the village. If everything else fails, the activists take the woman to their own homes and help her to get a divorce and remarry. "Recently, I had three such women in my house," says Palejo.

It is such personal help that wins the organisation a committed membership. "Sindhiani Tehrik saved my life," says Mariam Gopang, a thin 19-year-old from Lowari Sharif in Badin district. Gopang first met the Sindhiani women some years ago when nine members of her family were killed in a feud over a religious title. Sindhiani members visited the village and consoled the family. After that, they kept in touch with Gopang. When she finished high school, Gopang's father and brothers wanted her to stop studying. But with Sindhiani's support she continued her education. The family tried to marry her off to a twice-married man of 60. But she escaped, married a sympathetic cousin and is now a member of the organisation's central committee. Gopang's sister, Shahin, is also a member of Sindhiani. Her husband was killed in the village massacre and she lives on her own, supporting her young son. She has refused to wed any of the men her parents tried to thrust on her. "I will only marry this time of my own free will," says Shahin determinedly.

Whether it is a case of marriage or wife-beating, Sindhiani, with its elected committees at the taluka (sub-district), district and central levels, is mostly concerned with local issues. "The issues which preoccupy city women are very different from the ones that affect us," says Sheikh. "For example, what relevance does the urban women's agitation against the government's Hudood ordinance, which prescribes strict punishment for adultery or sex outside marriage, have for women who are governed by customs which are far stricter?"

Farm women find a forum
Imrana Khwaja

Lahore — Peasant women in this Islamic nation, who rarely leave their homes except to work in the fields, are slowly beginning to speak up. Defying their menfolk's anger, scores of peasant women left their children and work in November 1991 to meet for the first time in the history of this 44-year-old nation.

"People kept telling me that it wouldn't be possible to have such a conference in an orthodox country like Pakistan," says Chandni Joshi of UNIFEM (the United Nations Development Fund for Women), which sponsored the peasant women's meeting. "Despite enormous pressure from male members of their families, these women left work and children to attend the meeting." The conference, organised by a women's organisation, Aurat Foundation, was an eye-opener to the women from villages all over this country. "We thought we were the only ones who suffered, that the government had forgotten us," said Bibi Sultana, "but now I realise we aren't alone. Our hardships are common to all the peasant women of Pakistan."

Sultana, a large, gentle woman from the northern valley of Gilgit (on the ancient silk route from Pakistan to China), had never stepped out of her village before. Yet she spoke with confidence and her words came from the heart: "It is a great shame that though we live in an Islamic republic, we are suffering such oppression at the hands of the rulers. Until we get organised our voices will not be heard and our problems will be disregarded."

About 100 women like Sultana met in Manawan village on the outskirts of Lahore city in the first week of November to share their experiences. Gathered under a large tent, women speaking at least five different languages exchanged experiences about their work and problems, discussed possible solutions, and were given an opportunity to speak to politicians and policy makers. Many, like Sultana, had never stepped outside their villages in their entire lives, and were a little lost on arrival. But within a day they were sitting on a raised platform, microphone before them, articulating their problems as if they had been born to public speaking. Said one unlettered woman from Sindh, who had spoken with a power and conviction which would be the envy of any politician: "We have lived with these problems all our lives. Who can talk of them better than us?"

At first, participants spoke cautiously. Degeneration of forest resources, the main agenda of the meeting, emerged as a common problem. Hours of the peasant woman's day is spent in search of wood for fuel. The scarcity is most acute in the picturesque northern mountains where there is little alternative fuel. "Women are forced to climb for miles up steep slopes to get wood; and tourists take photographs of them as they scale trees, desperate to break off branches," said an indignant woman from the North West Frontier Province.

"Sometimes we have nothing but the cardboard in our caps to burn for fuel," Sultana said, pointing to her round, raised cap. Things are worse in the barren western province of Baluchistan. "Trees could be planted but where is the water for them ? There is hardly any water for people and animals to drink," complained a woman from the region.

Once the ice was broken, it was obvious that the women were angry about the government's failure to provide health care and education. And they were not afraid to openly voice this anger. As Rehmat Bibi, a thin grey-haired woman of about 60 from the Frontier province, said: "No one has mentioned these things yet. Are they afraid ? Well, I am not afraid. We are being oppressed by ministers, members of parliament, by the government." Women die in childbirth because there is not even a midwife in the villages. Meanwhile the politicians build big houses and factories. Where has the money come from ? The zakat committee (religious charity) members come look-ing extremely pious, make promises, take down names and disappear. To get the job of a messenger one needs the recommendation of a minister — ordinary people like us can't even get near a minister," she pointed out.

"The rich only remember the poor when it comes to elections; my province has been ruined at their hands," added Rose Bibi of Baluchistan.

For most peasant women the day begins at dawn, with housework and the search for fuel and water besides work in the fields, whether their own or the landlord's. "The landlord's wife forces us to work in her house and pays nothing; our children are dragged out of school to work on their fields. And the landlord tells us to bring our daughters to work in his house but his intentions are dubious," said Parveen from Bahawalpur in Punjab province. It was clear the women were only too well aware of the problems. The solutions, on the other hand, were not easy to find. By the end of three days some women were convinced of the importance of organising but there was too little time to go into details of how they could do so by themselves. Many others were already working in cooperatives through credit schemes, some of them extremely successful ones.

But the conference was not entirely a shot in the dark. Explained Joshi, "Similar conferences have been held in India and Nepal and one is due in Bangladesh in December. Then women from each of these countries will be invited to attend a regional conference in Lahore and some will be chosen to help formulate national conservation strategies." "Our intention is to take the concerns of rural women to the legislators and policy making bodies," said Nigar Ahmed of the Aurat Foundation.

Interestingly, only 24 of the 100 women assembled belonged to a women's organisation with a political perspective: the Sindhani Tehrik (Sindhi Women's Movement), affiliated to the Awami Tehrik (People's Movement).

Whether a government consisting largely of the landowning aristocracy would listen to them or not, the women are clear about one thing. As Mumtaz Rizamani, president of the Sindhiani Tehrik, said at the conclusion of the meeting: The worst part of women's oppression is that we accept it as natural. But we have the power to change it. The government of Pakistan will not do it for us, nor will any funding from far off places. The women of Pakistan should rely on themselves and no one else."

SRI LANKA

Tackling environmental issues
Vijita Fernando

Colombo — Vivacious Shantha works as a factory hand, packing insecticides for a privately owned company in Sri Lanka's capital, Colombo. She is happy there and is busy saving money to get married later this year. She is blissfully ignorant of the hazards of working with insecticides.

"There are 350 people working in this situation," says Duleep Jayamanne, Director of Occupational Hygiene of the Department of Labour. "There can be serious mutagenic and carcinogenic ill effects, especially for women working with insecticides," he warns. According to him the 50,000 women working in the Greater Colombo Economic Commission and the Free Trade Zone within it are at special risk for they not only work in an unhealthy environment, they also live in one.

Deafness can be caused by the noise in the factories, especially in textile units where looms are used, he points out. Even working with wood-shavings, foam, pulp and packing waste has hazards, he says. The Department of Labour and his division in particular is training volunteers who will work with government officials in assessing factory hazards for men and women. Several forms of control are being introduced and environment units are being set up to deal with offenders, says Jayamanne.

Industrial hazards are not the only environmental problem that government agencies and non-governmental organizations are currently concerned with in Sri Lanka. The Environment Foundation points out that major government sponsored schemes in the countryside also have their ecological cost. For instance, the Mahaweli Development Programme, a huge irrigation, power and resettlement project, neglected any environmental planning. Comments Kamini Vitarane of the Environment Foundation, "This is a case of lopsided planning. Trees have been cut down wholesale to make room for agriculture. Women are the worst affected by the resulting shortages of water and firewood. They must band together, like the women of India's Chipko movement, and protect the few trees that are left." (One of the ways the women of the Chipko movement raised grassrooots environmental consciousness in the mid-1970's was by hugging trees to prevent their felling by lumber companies.)

Chandra Hewagallage of the Community Education Centre, a non-governmental organization which works with women in the Mahaweli villages elaborates, "In the highly populated project area there is a water shortage. The purana gamas (old villages) have no water. The only source left are the streams. Here too there may be water only at the mouth of the stream and there are usually crowds bathing at such spots. Firewood too is scarce. Trees are cut down without thought. A little forest is left in Kotagala and everyone goes there for firewood. Only Suriyagama has no water problem. There UNICEF has provided wells — one well for seven or eight families.

The Environment Foundation has launched an awareness programme for schools and other agencies. It is particularly concerned with the lack of knowledge about laws relating to the environment and is collaborating with other groups to set up legal aid clinics to take up issues such as the legal right to protest against noise pollution caused by saw mills and rice mills.

Women are part of most environment campaigns. Padmini Abeywardena, Coordinator of the Centre for Women's Research Project, funded by the Dutch Embassy, says, "We have to tackle the degradation of the environment at the most basic level and we are starting with the women. They are closest to the environment and suffer the direct impact of ecological destruction." The project will study fuel saving, smoke reducing and cost effective cooking stoves and promote their use in rural areas and urban shanties. The aim is to reduce domestic drudgery for women.

Sumudu Luyanage, law officer of the Foundation, says, "As a first step we have published the rights enshrined in the Environment Act in Sinhala and Tamil language newspapers We are also making an attempt to have environment law introduced as a subject in the law college." The government's Central Environment Authority was only an advisory body until the beginning of the 1980s. As development led to environmental problems, awareness grew and various groups raised such a clamour that the Environment Act was amended. The agency now has powers to stop any project that endangers the environment. Impact assessment procedures have been formulated for new projects.

A.K.Gunawala, Director of Environmental Promotion, says, "This year we are concentrating on two areas. One is the effect of industrial effluents on women, the other is on the relation-ship of rural women and their lifestyle to the environment." Several agencies are involved in assessing the impact of environmental destruction. In recent years there has been a series of landslides, soil erosion, large scale deforestation, drying up of waterways, and pollution leading to fish poison-ing. These are current areas for concern and action by government and non-governmental bodies.

How green is my village
Vijita Fernando

Colombo — Nature has not been particularly kind to this tiny village in Sri Lanka's arid north central zone. Water is scarce and sanitation does not exist. Fifty-year-old Sriyaa has seen children die of diarrhoea, malnutrition and bouts of malaria that periodically attack her village. But in the past two years women like Sriyaa have had a glimpse of a different way of life. Last year a tubewell gushed forth precious water and a promise of greenery. This year some families have built toilets. And this is only the beginning. As the island's oldest rural women's organisation, Lanka Mahila Samithi (LMS) takes up an environ-mental programme, other changes are round the corner.

The LMS volunteers are no ordinary social workers but trek through jungles, braving landmines in a region close to the battle line between the country's Sinhala majority and the separatist Tamil minority. An occasional attack by militants is not uncommon in these parts. "It's a tough job," admits Yasawathi Sittarage, LMS coordinator for the region. But even tougher than the trek through jungles is the actual work in the villages. Convincing mothers that the precious drops of water they take hours to collect from boreholes need to be boiled before drinking is a tough task. Equally difficult is the job of convincing overworked mothers that they must prevent mosquitoes from breeding near their homes to fight malaria".

But it's a sign of the headway made by the LMS in the region that villagers invariably welcome Sriyaa and other LMS workers with a hot cup of tea, and linger for a chat. There is nothing they do not confide to an LMS worker. "We talk to them about the baby's worms, the children's lack of books. We even tell them when our husbands drink," says a young villager, Nalini.

It took 60 years of hard work for the LMS to build this trust. Part of the reason why rural women are not overawed by the organisation is because most LMS workers are villagers like themselves, who have been trained at the LMS centre in Kaduwela, near the capital Colombo. The women, chosen for their leadership qualities, learn about improving the environment, providing safe water and sanitation. They also learn how to cook healthier meals for their families, and they pick up some job skills as well. The idea is that they take this wealth of new information back to their villages to share with their neighbours. A network of field coordinators, supervised by a team of organisers, monitor their progress. All work is voluntary, except for travel stipends given to field workers like Yasawathi.

The LMS started the environment health programme a year ago. Backed by the Central Environment Authority and UNICEF, its thrust so far has been on safe domestic water, food safety, solid waste disposal and vector control. Behind it are dynamic organisers like Malini Jayasekera who recently retired from the Government School of Agriculture. "Providing the software of environmental sanitation is our job,"she says. "Health education must start, for instance, before toilets are sited. By the time the toilets are ready, users must be aware of the need to keep them clean, washed and free from flies." Jayasekara is only too well aware of how difficult it is for poor families to follow even basic rules of hygiene. "Eking out a living, educating children, coping with bouts of illness and still having the goodness of a balanced diet at the back of their heads when putting together a skimpy meal is not easy," she admits.

However, women are slowly beginning to see the link between a healthy environment and their family's health. As Anoja Fernando, president of LMS, says They are grasping the importance of this benign cycle of a cleaner environment, of turning garbage into fertiliser, using it in home gardens to provide nutritious food for the family and, as a bonus, selling some vegetables and using the money for the children's schoolbooks . . . "Other LMS workers agree that the programme has worked wonders in a year. Even in areas of extreme rural poverty there is some glimmer of hope," points out Gunawardhana, a field coordinator whose work spreads over 20 villages. She is one of the 25 senior coordinators who work with 547 rural women and reach out through them to 12,000 households.

Coordinators like Gunawardhana are crucial to the success of the programme. For their training, says Fernando, LMS networked with the Central Environment Authority, the Health Department, the National Water Supply and Drainage Board and the Colombo Municipality. The three-month course trained 90 coordinators in 28 training courses for nearly 600 members of rural committees. Fourteen districts were covered in the first phase. Each branch of LMS takes 30 households through a step by step training in environmental health. The women also get the whole village to do voluntary work in building roads or clearing the jungle.

Encouraged by the programme's success, UNICEF now plans to induce villagers to make other changes in their lifestyle: get families to use mosquito nets treated with repellents, set aside different wells for drinking water, for washing and bathing in order to avoid pollution, build makeshift shelves of coconut leaves to store water above floor level, use food covers made of local materials, use fuel efficient stoves and dig garbage and compost pits in every garden.

Protecting trees, of course, is not the problem in this Buddhist majority island that it has become elsewhere. Planting and tending trees comes easily even in this arid region because here reverence for trees is rooted in religion.

NGOs woo women with water
Vijita Fernando

Colombo — Five years ago many rural folk in Sri Lanka were passive beneficiaries of aid programmes that provided services like water and sanitation to communities. Now they are partners in the process. The breakthrough came with the pioneering efforts of a few NGOs.

"We found," says Mala Liyanage, project coordinator of the Sri Lanka Mahila Samithi, "that rural women were always responsive when water or sanitation were mentioned . They usually turned up at meetings on these. Earlier, nothing would get them out." The Mahila Samiti decided to try out a comprehensive project in Moneragala, in the extreme south of the country. Women volunteers were trained to conduct a survey of the 140 village families, note the condition of existing toilets and water sources and identify prospective beneficiaries.

Several meetings later the women were taught to draw a map of the village and mark the sites of the toilets and wells. Next, they learnt to bank the money available for the project, began keeping accounts and met officials of the Ministry of Health to get subsidised concrete slabs for the toilets they planned to build. "They were the programme managers and monitored the work. Some were actual bricklayers and masons and combined these roles with those of monitor/evaluators," says Liyanage.

Over the months, the women have gained new status in the village. They control the use of water sources and specify bathing days for men and women at they community bathing well. They demand that buckets and ropes be kept clean and have few inhibitions about meeting men and discussing things with them. "Our men are at last getting used to it," smiles Ariwathie, one of the leaders of the project.

In Kitulawa, a village south of Colombo, a mother's club recruited women for health education classes when they arrived at mid-morning to collect their children from the preschool. The women were taught the importance of sanitation and clean drinking water in keeping their families healthy. With the help of the Girl Guides' Association they promoted a health campaign in this village of 250 families. The Association provided 100 toilets for the community. At the same time, under a UNICEF/Ministry of Health water project, six wells were dug, with women providing the labour for one of them.

"Six months later there were problems in the wells due to rusting of pipes. But the toilets were in mint condition due to the women's efforts at maintenance," says Padmini Amerasinghe who coordinated the project for the Guides. It was not easy for village women to get involved in community work. "We had a lot of trouble from the men when we first tried to join the mothers' club and get active," says Tilaka, 22. Her taxi-driver husband was away from home a good deal and time hung heavily on her hands. "But it took my mother-in-law to convince him that I should join the group," she says.

The Sarvodaya story goes back to the beginning of the decade, when this large NGO collaborated with the International Development and Research Centre (IDRC) of Canada to develop a handpump design for developing countries. "As rural women are the main group who suffer because of shortage of potable water, we felt they should play a more important role in our efforts," says Claudia Iddamalgoda who documented the programme.

The pilot project started off with the selection of 20 women in Padiyatalawa, a village deep in the dry zone. Ten were trained for two months on all aspects of well construction and the other 10 in planning, fitting, welding, lathework and smithwork or manufacturing the handpumps. This was rounded off with training in assembling the handpump, monitoring, maintenance and evaluation. The training has continued in batches over the last six years. Trained women now maintain handpumps in 12 villages in the dry zone. "Our first difficulties were in selecting the women. Objections came from the men who felt that technical work was not for women," says Iddamalgoda.

Now the story is different. "We have no more problems with

water," says Nandawathie, a veteran trained in the first batch. "When the handpumps go out of order we don't have to wait for our men to come home. They are now accepting that we can do this job as well as any other."

"Mothers are our first priority," observes Sisira Kumarasiri, field coordinator of the German Agency for Technical Development. This agency implements a massive water/sanitation programme in Karunegala district, in the rain-scarce northwest. "It is the mothers who fetch water from the water source, manage and control it in times of scarcity. Their domestic life revolves round water. We have taken this into serious account in every phase of our project," says Kumarasiri.

Ironically the total involvement of women with water sometimes works against the interests of communities. Mothers tend to pass on false beliefs and myths about water. Boiling drinking water is unacceptable to most rural folk here. They believe boiled water is 'dead' and that flowing water with the sun shining on it is best for drinking. "Warm water is only for the very old or sick. It has no taste. Healthy people don't drink boiled water," a woman of Kitulawa said, responding to a survey sponsored by UNDP in 1986.

Traditional water sources are considered sacred in Sri Lanka and their water is used in folk ceremonies. This creates resistance to new wells, especially to tubewells whose water source is hidden. Older women tend to go back to traditional sources after the initial thrill of a new supply.

Some traditional beliefs do contain time-tested truths but many are harmful. "Women have the biggest role in providing safe water. They are also the chief offenders," comments a doctor attached to the National Institute of Health Service in Kalutara.

PHILIPPINES

Growing rich and green
Elsie K. Santos

Manila — Charley Barretto ought to be in the Guinness Book of Records. She is known in the Philippines as "the woman who planted a million trees in just 730 days".

Barretto is the founder of the World Ecologists (WE) Foundation, a non-profit organisation dedicated to conserving natural resources, improving the environment and maintaining the ecological balance in the Philippines. Each year about 105,000 hectares of Philippine forests are stripped of their cover. Much of the blame is placed on licensed loggers but slash-and-burn farmers, forest fires, pests, diseases and illegal logging aggravate the problem. The government has increased the budget for reforestation in 1990 to nearly US$ 10 million, but the Department of Environment and Natural Resources says this is a small amount, considering the extent of deforestation.

Since it was launched two years ago, WE has initiated innovative campaigns that attack the most basic environmental problems. Punong Yaman (the term means both "full of wealth" and "tree of wealth") is a livelihood project that provides organisations seeds, soil and fertilisers with which to start nurseries.

Participants in the project raise seeds. Their only investment is plastic bags. WE buys the seedlings when they are about half a metre high and ready for re-planting. Punong Yaman is part of WE's plan to fill public lands with trees, especially fruit-bearing ones. The foundation invests hundreds of thousands of pesos in buying seedlings from nurseries. WE's volunteer planters, mostly women, leave their jobs two days a month to go where their services are needed.

The 59 centres now involved in Punong Yaman include the Golden Acres home for the aged, orphanages, military camps and squatter resettlement projects of the government. Boso-Boso in the mountainous town of Antipolo just outside of Manila is a Punong Yaman showcase. When WE introduced the project in the village only three or four landless farmers showed some interest. The rest of the community were reluctant to join because they had been disappointed by the lack of follow-up of similar government programmes in the past. What slowly won them over was the enthusiasm of the WE members in negotiating the rocky uphill roads leading to their village and the incomes the project generated for the first participants.

One of them, Rolando Salvador, collected almost US$ 200 for the jackfruit and "alibangbang" seedlings he grew. With his first earnings he was able to cement the floor of his house and buy a secondhand television set. Another farmer, Danilo Prendol, bought two pigs and hollow blocks to complete his house with his income from Punong Yaman. Ben and Felicidad Fausto used the money for their two children's schooling.

Lydia Avila, Punong Yaman chairperson, encourages the farmers to scour their area for fallen seeds from neighbouring trees so that they do not depend solely on the fruit seeds collected through WE campaigns. Last year, with 59 Punong Yaman centres requiring seeds, WE started a seed collection campaign in schools. The campaign is making school children aware of the need to care for their environment by saving the seeds of the fruits they eat at home. The seeds they collect are given to the foundation and planted in school grounds and other public land. WE's tree planting project has been dubbed "fruitopia" and covers 50 sites, including watersheds, military camps, school grounds and highways.

The military is among its most active supporters. At one camp in Tanay, a hilly town two hours by car from Manila, the soldiers picked up shovels and planted more than 20,000 seedlings along the denuded hills. Employees of the Philippines national railways have planted half a million seedlings along the 600-km stretch of tracks spanning north to south. The seedlings are being nurtured by the employees themselves who, along with the slum communities living near the tracks, will enjoy the fruits the trees will bear.

WE's latest project links patriotism with protection of the environment. Called the "Iba na ang Filipino" movement ("the Filipino is different now") it requires its members to wear Filipino attire, speak Filipino, listen to Filipino music, eat Filipino food and buy a Filipino product every Friday. The idea may sound inane, but not in a country where western cultural influences are firmly entrenched at all socio-economic levels. WE hopes that by learning to care deeply for Filipino things, its members will better understand why they must care even more for their environment.

Since the movement was launched last June, it has enlisted more than a hundred corporate groups. Its volunteers include beauticians, nutritionists at a government hospital, salesgirls, and business executives. WE leaders have started meeting with members of Congress to get them to introduce a bill that would make mandatory the nationwide observance of Filipino Day every Friday.

"Never ask what a tree can do," says founder Barretto. "Just plant it and see. And the next time someone asks how soon we can solve our ecological problems, ask him or her, how soon can you plant a tree?"

Children crusade for the forests
Lorna Kalaw-Tirol

Manila — An environmental activist, tired of waiting for government to act decisively on the worsening depletion of Philippine forests, is suing it on behalf of 39 children, three of them his own. Antonio Oposa, a 35-year-old lawyer based in Makati, the country's financial centre, filed the unprecedented class action with the regional trial court in April 1990. Named as petitioners in the suit are his three young children, the eldest a three-year-old boy and the youngest, a mere infant, and the children of associates and friends who share his alarm over the Philippines' ecological future.

All the children are under 17.

"These children represent their generation and generations yet unborn," Oposa explains. He says he worries that by the time his eldest child is 15 the Philippines will have no forests left. It is the children who will directly suffer the consequences, he points out.

Since last year Oposa and his wife, Rizalina, have been rallying their friends to their cause. That was not too difficult to do. What was more difficult was getting the Department of Environment and Natural Resources (DENR) to take seriously Oposa's demand, contained in a letter to Secretary Fulgencio Factoran Jr, that his office cancel all the logging permits it has granted.

Since 1989 the Philippines senate has been embroiled in a passionate debate over logging, with its members divided between those who advocate a total ban and those who prefer a selective ban. The issue of logging is an urgent one for the Philippines. Twenty-five years ago out of its 30 million hectares, 16 million were virgin rain forests. In 1987 satellite images showed that no more than 1.2 million hectares remained. Last year the number was further reduced to about 900,000 hectares.

"Yet we continue to cut at the rate of 150,000 to 200,000 hectares a year," fumes Oposa. He himself does not favour a total log ban which he says would dislocate hundreds of thousands of Filipinos dependent on the wood industry, as well as the furniture and construction industries. What he would rather see, he says, is a total prohibition on cutting down virgin and secondary growth forests: the first because too few remain and the second because they must be allowed to regenerate. However, Oposa qualifies, industrial tree planta-tions and tree farms may be allowed to utilise the commercial species of wood derived from the farms on plantations, but these must be used only by the domestic market.

Oposa's suit asks the court to cancel all existing timber licence arrangements in the country and to order the DENR to desist from receiving, accepting, processing, reviewing or approving new agreements. He blames the current situation on politics, saying, "So much has already been said on the issue, but very little has been done. Both political branches of government, the executive and the legislature appear to be indecisive, foot-dragging, compromising or simply helpless. They are highly vulnerable to the influence of powerful and well-oiled vested interests." He adds, "There is nothing personal in this action, it is not Factoran we are fighting, but his office."

So friendly is the case, to use Oposa's words, that before going to court he informed Factoran of his move. The secretary, Oposa claims, encouraged him to go ahead and welcomed the suit as a chance for his office to talk about its accomplishments as well as the constraints it has to work under. "What we want to happen is to bring the issue to a head, to encourage debate on it. If you file a case on behalf of children it becomes more dramatic. It makes people ask questions,"

In the United States where he went to meet with other environmental activists shortly after filing the case, he was repeatedly told that the suit was unprecedented in the world: the first to involve children and to be nationwide in scope. Oposa is more than ever convinced that "We don't have to destroy to make money," referring to the destruction of entire forests to generate dollars for the Philippines economy.

At the trial he plans to present a well-known local artist who will show that out of a small piece of wood he can sculpt a work of art that can fetch more than the cost of thousands of boards exported as timber. Another alternative he suggests is the development of eco-tourism which, he says, has been found to be successful in countries like Kenya whose game preserves have been drawing in thousands of tourists.

Asked if the court case would prosper, Oposa replies, "As a cocky lawyer, I say it will," but he expects to be confronted with technical questions such as the legal right of the children to sue. However he says the Department of Environment has assured him that it will not raise technicalities against the case. "At least in the court we have an impartial tribunal where we can be dispassionate about the issue,".

Whether or not he will have his day in court, Oposa already feels gratified that he has done his duty as a parent. "Ecological gangrene cannot be healed by a legislative band- aid," he asserts. "We need something stronger and more painful to arrest the unabated plunder of our natural resource treasures and the continued rape of mother earth."

A return to nature
Sylvia L. Mayuga

Manila — Elin Belamide Mondejar's grandfather fought in the Philippines Revolution of 1898 against the Spaniards. The sense of family pride helped her to return to traditional Filipino ways that are gradually dying out in the Philippines.

It runs in the family. Mondejar's mother, Elisea Kiamson Belamide, founded the Cavite Institute, a secondary school with a strong science curriculum for farm children, in Cavite province just outside Manila. This school became Mondejar's home base for a deepening involvement with rural poverty, malnutrition and disease.

Like her mother and most other rural activists in the late 1960s and early 1970s, Mondejar started off by educating and organising farmers for agrarian reform. But working closely with farmers revealed a truth she had never before realised — the burden imposed on farmers by the green revolution with the nationwide switch from organic to chemical farming.

Mondejar found that most farmers were worried about repaying the loans they were forced to take to buy imported fertilisers and pesticides; most farmers' co-operatives were very concerned about repaying these loans, especially when the 'miracle' rice crops failed and there was nothing to pay with. Mondejar saw rice crops totally ruined by the dreaded tungro disease in Saint Maria, in the neighbouring province of Laguna. Studies by the International Rice Research Institute (IRRI) based in Laguna later revealed that the leafhopper pest increased because chemicals also destroyed its natural enemies.

"Working with the farmers," says Mondejar, "we realised that the land itself was being destroyed."

The farmers' disenchantment with the green revolution was later voiced at international conferences and in books like Rachel Carson's *Silent Spring,*. and Robert Van Den Bosch's *Pesticide Conspiracy*. The discovery of research grants for the IRRI funded by multinationals producing chemicals for the monoculture of rice fuelled the controversy. Alternatives had to be found for expensive technologies sold to 'client states'like the Philippines, and there was no better place to find them than in its own traditions.

In 1978, Mondejar prodded the Cavite Institute to conduct a study by its students on upland rice varieties and indigenous farming practices in the province. They discovered that 50 such varieties raised for home consumption as late as the 1950s and 1960s had dwindled to 10 varieties in the 1970s, thanks to the 'green revolution' and the spreading cash crop economy. Another study 10 years later found that all these varieties had vanished from Silang town.

In 1980, the Cavite Institute, together with another non-governmental organisation bought a 2.9 hectare experimental farm, which managed to save some of the upland rice varieties found in 1978. The Cavite Experimental Station (CREST) became a community seed-bank, exchanging seeds and information throughout the country and as far as Sarawak and Sri Lanka.

A world conference on primary health care, called by the World Health Organisation (WHO) in Alma-Ata in the USSR in 1978, provided another angle on the misery of rural populations in the Third World: the prohibitive cost of health care.

By now CREST had given rise to a second organisation called IDEAS (Institute for the Development of Educational and Ecological Alternatives). In 1986, it helped organise a consultation in Manila with experts from. six other Third World countries on the international sharing of appropriate technology. Discussions focused on, among other things, the potential of herbal medicines, which are cheap compared to multinational drugs.

Mondejar joined forces with Paulina Javier, the school principal, and Gladys Dichoso, an outstanding chemistry student. Together, they encouraged students to gather and study local medicinal herbs. They learnt that Silang had a living herbal tradition. Each village had as many as six practitioners of herbal medicine. They also found a valuable ally in Volita Amiscosa, science supervisor of the Department of Education. She encouraged 200 public schools in Cavite to plant medicinal herb gardens. In a year medicinal herb scrapbooks were collected and their findings summarised in a directory listing 379 species found in Cavite. An initial pharmacopoeia has also been published of 100 medicinal plants for common ailments.

The herbal medicine campaign stimulated a new ecological awareness. Last year, at the first observance of International Earth Day in the Philippines, 3000 people gathered at the Silang town plaza for a grassroots celebration. It sparked off a campaign on saving the local rivers.

Consciousness is spreading. In the town of Bacoor, officials are discussing a plan to save their own river. Among their first ideas is an educational campaign on non bio-degradable plastics that clog rivers the world over.

Giant project threatens farmers
Sol Juvida

Cavite — Project Calabarzon, a 735 million dollar government industrialisation programme for southern Luzon, has been attracting major investors since its inception in 1989. It has also been stirring up a storm of protests from small farmers whose lands will be lost in the process of industrialisation.

Calabarzon stands for Cavite, Laguna, Batangas and Rizal — all southern Tagalog provinces included in the nation's 10-year industrialisation programme with a budget of 19.3 billion pesos (US$ 735 million). The government has lined up 46 projects for port, road, communication development and power generation. So far, the project can count on an investment of 30.9 billion pesos (US$1.17 billion).

Calabarzon aims to transform southern Luzon, the largest among 14 regions in the country, into an attractive site for a high-tech industrial centre that will create jobs and increase rural income. However, Calabarzon is mainly an agricultural region. More than half of southern Luzon's labour force are engaged in agricultural work producing staple food and commercial crops such as coconut, sugarcane, rice, coffee, vegetables, fruits and nuts.

The project is also considered a good opportunity for both the government and the private sector to be able to solve much of the problem now besetting metro Manila, such as congestion, traffic, waste disposal and environmental degradation. Major investors will be mostly Japanese transnational corporations like Mitsubishi, Marubeni, Mitsui, Kawasaki and their subsidiaries, as well as local big capitalists.

However, critics are pointing out that the government can only promise some 340,000 new jobs out of the project, whereas at least 4.4 million people are likely to be displaced by it. Moreover, it is hardly certain that the project would generate genuine industrialisation because what foreign investors want to put up are processing and assembly plants. The few factory jobs that will become available are cold comfort for the hundreds of thousands of farmers who would lose their lands in the process.

Spearheading the protest is the Congress for People's Agrarian Reform, a coalition of progressive peasants associations in the Philippines, who maintain that industrialisation and agriculture should go hand in hand, and one should not be sacrificed for the other. In Cavite, a two-hour drive from Manila, farmers have organised themselves against Project Calabarzon although some have already "sold out" to the government and private investors.

Land ownership remains a thorny issue in Cavite, where generations of small farmers have been working on lands owned by landlords. According to the land reform programme of the government, farmers can apply for ownership of lands they have been tilling for years. But farmers in Calabarzon are compelled, under current government orders, to sell their lands for the project at the prevailing market prices.

Of the six barangays or villages in Silang in Cavite province, two have already sold out to the government. The other four however, have not felt any pressure from the government so far.

"They will try to buy us out last," says Teresita Alvarez of Tartaria village, who heads a women farmers group in Silang, a major industrial site under the project. In Alvarez' village, which under the project will be the site of a low-cost housing project, nearly half the households are organising themselves to stand up against Project Calabarzon. Last year, for instance, several women formed a mothers' group to learn more about the project.

According to Alvarez, a young mother of three, some 30 mothers from her village formed "ugnayan ng mga ina" (mothers' association) to protest against Project Calabarzon and its effects on their farms, their means of livelihood and their environment. Although the group is small, their grim determination is a real threat to the local landlords who want to sell out to either the government or private investors. Once, for instance, the landlords sent bulldozers to break the human barricade the women had formed on the farms. But the bulldozers did not daunt the women, who kept standing in front of the giant machines and forced the bulldozers to retreat from the scene.

Like many farmers in this region, Alvarez and her husband have a six-acre farm where they grow everything from coffee and pineapples to bananas and rootcrops. The farm has been in the family through generations, dating from the time of the Spanish colonists.

Alvarez is proud of their new crop of "some 1,000 heads of pineapple," which they can harvest in 18 months. But they are hardly sufficient to make ends meet. "What with the rising cost of fertilisers and everything, we have to borrow money," she says.

They also raise pigs, chickens and cows to supplement their meagre income. But despite the hard life, Alvarez and her family find it impossible to think of leaving their farm. "If we allow ourselves to be driven out now, we'll also be driven away from other lands in the future,"she points out, adding: "What about the future of our children? That's why we have organised ourselves for we are not going to leave this place. Our parents were born and died on this land, and so will we."

Alvarez is not the only woman leader in the province. In Langkaan village in Dasmarinas, 64-year-old Damaza Perez is also helping farmers to protest against their imminent displacement. Langkaan is a beautiful, hilly land of orchards and paddy fields. Like Silang, the cool climate is most suitable for growing a variety of fruits and vegetables.

Last year, Perez led a group of women and children against a group of men carrying out a landlord's order. The landlord, who wanted to switch over to sugarcane in his fields and plans to have factories built nearby, had ordered the men to plough his fields with a tractor in preparation for the sugarcane plantation. "Nanay Masang", or Mother Masang as Perez is affectionately called by the villagers, led a group of women and children against the tractor drivers.

The women and children were the only ones in the village at that time because all the men had left the village on the same day to appeal to the department of agrarian reforms against the order. They formed a barricade, hauling cart wheels and big stones onto the middle of the road. They managed to stop the tractors, a victory so unexpected that Nanay Masang and her band of women and children felt spurred on to fight against Project Calabarzon.

But Nanay Masang realises only too well how unequal the fight against the project is going to be. Already half of Langkaan has been sold to the project, at an astronomical 300,000 pesos (US$ 11,407) per hectare. But Perez is determined to fight to the finish. "We need the land. We don't want the money, which just gets spent fast," she says.

Perez inherited her small piece of land from her parents. She and her husband, who died a few years ago of snakebite, raised their nine children on the income they made from the farm. "Here there is no way one can go hungry," explains Perez, as she sits down with her family to a meal of rice and bitter gourd sauted in fish flakes. "There are always vegetables around that we can gather and cook."

According to Perez, the hardest part about leaving their land is not knowing what the future holds for them. "It will be hard for us to transfer from this fertile land to another land that we are not familiar with," she sighs. "The government seems to have forgotten us." Although her village is only an hour's ride from Manila, it still has no electricity or running water. That is why, she feels, organisations like hers help farmers to help themselves. For instance, it was able to loan money to young farmers to buy rice threshers, among other things.

Like the negligence of the government, Perez is not prepared to submit to the powerful project. "I told the man who was pointing his gun at me that I'm not afraid of bullets because they can kill you fast," she says, recalling what she told those men accompanying the bulldozers. "I am more afraid of hunger. It kills you slowly."

Latin America

"When I saw the people living in those skyscrapers, I thought, they must be very sad people up there, so far from the earth, so far from their roots."

— Statement by a Piaroa indigenous
leader from the Venezuelan Amazon

ENVIRONMENTAL DESTRUCTION AND Latin America's historical role as a source of raw materials, both have their roots in the specific development of global interdependence, initiated 500 years ago with the Spanish expansion and colonization of the American continent. One might, in fact, go so far as to say that it is precisely the concept of 'roots,' that acts as a connecting thread and enables an analysis of recent and past Latin American socio-economic evolution in environmental terms.

Latin American history is dominated by the different nations that have maintained hegemonic control over it, receiving raw materials in exchange for manufactured goods and technology. Spain and Portugal came first and were dominant until the seventeenth century, gradually losing ground to Great Britain, which held sway until the nineteenth, when the United States took over. The conquest of the Americas represents more than just another incarnation of colonialism: it enabled a massive transfer of wealth and natural resources that laid the foundation for European economic prosperity and its subsequent maritime expansion throughout Africa, Asia and the Pacific Islands. This expansionism, typified by nineteenth century England, consolidated a grid of intercontinental commerce and global economic interdependence, governed and administered by European empires via colonialism and mercantile monopolies.

Less than a century later, using colonial wealth to fuel an industrial revolution, European nations, joined by the United States and Japan, transformed traditional colonialism into a capitalist economic system that continues to control, harvest and deplete the stil rich natural resources of non-industrialised nations at a rate that has taken millions of people to the brink of poverty, and placed life on the planet in peril.

Uprooting

The arrival of Spanish conquistadors to America historically marks the beginning of the 'uprooting' and superceding of an indigenous culture and the introduction of others,and is embodied in one of the most merciless genocides and phenomenal migrations in human history — 13 million Africans brought to the Americas as slaves, 20 million indigenous people killed, and the arrival of more than 30 million European immigrants in less than three centuries.

A complete submergence of local cultures, however, was never accomplished; they managed to survive, while newer and mixed cultures emerged to shape the present Latin American ethos. Nevertheless, the impact of colonization on the indigenous population was determinant at all levels; the newcomers established a new status quo where the indigenous became the providers of labour, sustaining the economy of the colony from the bottom. For women, as always, this meant a further degrading of their already subordinate social position.

Women's portrayal in Latin American history, as in all the world, has always been nebulous because, whether in books or on stone, history has been inscribed only by men. Objects of worship through the many cults of mother goddess and mother earth, or sustainers of domestic hearth and agricultural field, women in indigenous cultures were crucial to sustaining life but had little impact on political or religious decision making.

The collision between the Spanish and the indigenous cultures inevitably introduced a third element, and it was, equally inevitably, women who by force or by will, became the bridge between the two, originating the 'mestizo' (mixed) culture through which the survival and dominion of Spanish and western presence in the region was ensured. At the material level, if one were to draw the links between environment, population, culture and history, women in the continent continued to be the providers of agricultural and domestic labour. Thus, as producers and reproducers, both, they carried the creation of a new culture forward.

The arrival of the Europeans to the continent meant the replacement of the indigenous cultural root- which considers 'humanity' as interdependent on nature and environment — by the westernized anthropocentric 'man', which sees nature as a source of raw materials to be processed for the furtherance of mankind's well-being and 'progress'.

After the consolidation of agriculture and mining as the main- stays of export in a mercantilist economic system, the heirs of the Spaniards rose against the 'metropolis' and, supported by the Principles and Rights of Man adopted in eighteenth century France, demanded independence from Spain as well as generated anti-slavery movements during in the nineteenth century.

The indigenous people, meanwhile, continued to fight for the preservation of their land, their autonomy and self-sufficiency through intermittent violent outbursts or passive resistance, first against the colonial empires and later against the socio-economic elite, military regimes and dictators that have peppered Latin American history.

After the Spanish domination receded, Latin America's social elite maintained the same colonial and economic power, based on a concentration of wealth and natural resources, while subjugating a massive labour force into processing the raw material for export. Industrialised nations continued to dictate their demands well into the nineteenth and twentieth centuries.

If Mexico and Venezuela export crude oil and petroleum

products, countries like Chile, Brazil, Argentina, Colombia, Peru and Bolivia combine the export of strategic minerals with grains, meat and other agricultural produce. Meanwhile, Central America and the Caribbean, which lack mineral resources, concentrate on large-scale mono-cropping of coffee, cotton, banana, and sugar for export, while exploiting their natural and geographic resources for importing tourists. Only a few countries like Brazil, Cuba and, to a certain extent, Argentina, Chile, Mexico and Venezuela have been able to develop technology and industry, although it is secondary and closely related to the processing of their raw materials.

While the exploitation and export of natural resources during the nineteenth century demanded an ever-increasing accumulation of land and resource rights by exporters, the majority of the people were relegated to the poorest and most inhospitable lands. This phenomenon is evident throughout Latin America, especially in the less industrialized countries of Bolivia, Guatemala, Paraguay and Peru, although bigger countries like Brazil and Mexico also followed the same logic. Moreover, because of the high concentration of resources, the only political administration which could hold this economic system in place was far from democratic; it emulated the former colonial mode, albeit in a new garb: the dictatorship, which appeared across the region during the twentieth century.

Thus, with its roots firmly embedded in extensive environmental exploitation, a systematic depletion of resources took place, with a growing number of forests and lands sacrificed for export. The consequent accumulation of financial resources by the Latin American economies allowed a quick passage to urbanization, and the incorporation of the region into the market economy promoted by western industrialization.

The implications of this for the survival of the indigenous and the local were alarming. Entire regions and countries have witnessed a degree of environmental ruin, drought and desertification that effectively stops their economies in their tracks. The once fertile north-eastern region of Brazil, which during the nineteenth century was the sugar capital of the country, is now drought-ridden, overpopulated and poverty-stricken. Such drastic—and unconscionable—measures as the forced sterilization of women and the elimination of street children by death-squads are a desperate response to a poverty created by excess.

It is on this site of ecological collapse that women are again the most vulnerable and impacted. While some landowners in Brazil may have 'fazendas' as large as the United Kingdom in order to breed cattle for export, or grow soya or any other cash crop for the same purpose, millions of Brazilians are forced to migrate to the Amazon region to burn the trees and the thin organic soil that covers the forest, without which it turns into a desert. It is no accident that in September 1991, around 300,000 women from the north-east gathered to defend the little forest available to them to collect the babacu nuts which grow in it; for those who possess no other resource, the only resource left is their hands. Landowners across the continent have only been able to respond with organized private armies, or military governments and the police, which have only produced political violence and death.

Hidden from general notice by the forests, is the pollution caused by mercury which is used by the garimpeiros (gold searchers) who flee from the most impoverished regions to look for any chance of survival. In this cycle, too, women become the poorest of the poor and the most harassed. Thousands of women are brought into prostitution, some from the time they are 11 years old, and are kept and used by the garimpeiros in camps hidden in the forest. Poor children too, are contracted from economically depressed areas to work in the gold-mining camps.

Displacing

Sadly, however, while phenomena like drought and forest destruction have become a matter of international debate and have been clearly identified as the effects of ecological destruction, other crucial aspects like increasing poverty and a sharp decline in living standards have not yet been linked to it. Indeed the most crucial and dramatic aspect of environmental harassment is its incapacity to satisfy the most fundamental needs of people —life, shelter and work— any more; its tragedy is the bitter fruit of dehumanization and disrespect for life, human or animal, that it brings in its wake. What hope survives, springs from the richness of grassroots movements fighting for social revival and change, typified by anonymous community workers and better-known political leaders like Luiza Erundina, the mayor of Sao Paolo, and a native and social product of the depressed north-east region of this country.

Apart from the long term economic stagnation and impoverishment caused by unbalanced distribution and exploitation of natural resources, capital accumulated in the richest countries was then directed to secondary industries devoted to processing the raw materials. Venezuela, for example, has abandoned almost all its agricultural production to focus on the petroleum industry, thus sparking off rapid urbanisation and migration to the cities in a mere six decades. This process finds echoes in several larger and smaller countries throughout the continent.

Moreover, the economic 'booms' caused by high prices for raw materials on the international market generated periods of economic prosperity that have given rise to a 'middle' or consumer class that, despite its social and economic dynamics, has not been able to break the economic cycle that keeps them dependent on technology and goods from abroad, while continuing to be the suppliers of raw material. When a country like Guatemala tried to extricate itself from it in the 1950s, with a democratically elected government (supported by the middle class and popular sectors) that advocated land reform and the development of an internal market and industrial capabilities, its efforts were smothered by the intervention of United Fruit Company, the CIA alliance with local military sectors, and the country's large landowners.

Many such economic 'booms' have marked the recent history of Latin America. World War II was particularly profitable for the region, when products like rubber, minerals, cattle and wheat made the fortunes of countries like Argentina, Brazil and many others, which provided food and raw materials to sustain the countries at war. Moreover, critical moments in the life of raw materials in the international market gave rise to periods of great prosperity. One such was the oil boom of the 70s which became an almost bottomless source of income for countries like Mexico and Venezuela. But the bonanza did not last long and many additional factors complicated the story of Latin America's evolution.

The wealth generated by the region during World War II encouraged newer social forces and innovative economic trends towards the promotion of a more diversified and dynamic economy, based on the development of local industry. At the same time, the needs of productive forces pushed women in to enter the labour market, while urban women took to higher education in large number. The participation of Latin American women in social and political structures was further encouraged by the right to vote which was generally obtained in the late forties.

In Brazil, President Getulio Vargas pushed for a model of national autonomous development to "replace the imports", but here again local power equations, forged by an agrarian economy and vested interests, conspired against the change. Once more, the active support of the United States in collusion with local military forces, ushered in the next phase in the history of the region: the revival of military dictatorships, this time within the framework of the Cold War and the doctrine of `National Security'. This was actively promoted by the U.S which barred the way to all democratic and innovative aspirations in most countries of the region: from the Central American republics to Uruguay, Brazil, Argentina and, later, Chile, whose populations payed a heavy tribute through the lives of women, men and children; Argentina and Guatemala, alone, claim a balance-sheet of 30,000 and 40,000 `disappeared' during their military regimes.

Resisting

The lack of political space and democratic expression gave birth to nationalist armed movements, later influenced by Marxism, in the late Fifties. With the exception of Cuba, and later

Nicaragua, these movements were unable to gain power, but they did engage in protracted civil 'wars' which claimed more than 200,000 lives in Guatemala, El Salvador and Nicaragua. With the exception of the peace accords reached in El Salvador, armed movements elsewhere continue to ravage the land. Conflict persists in Colombia and Guatemala, while in Peru, the Shining Path guerillas keep the grassroots movements and the army under the same fire.

Here again women have been strongly affected. The economic crisis in Peru encouraged the people, especially women, to look for alternative sources of survival; the creation of the popular canteens and the Glass of Milk committees, which offered basic meals to people who could not afford to cook at home, were among the more successful. But recent developments show up the authorities' failure not only in providing basic needs to the people, but in offering protection to those very women who were giving sustenance. The Glass of Milk committees came under constant fire from the Shining Path, and in February this year, one of the most popular and active leaders of this women's movement, Maria Elena Moyano, was shot down in cold blood by a Shining Path squad.

Still, movements for social change will not give up in this vibrant continent. Through the 1960s and 1970s, numerous movements were born, including the Catholic Liberation Theology, and scores of indigenous grassroots and other groups. Through a blending and intermingling of traditional religious roots — Catholic, Indigenous, African and Mestizo — with lay principles of human rights, leaders of these social movements for change are as diverse as Guatemalan human rights activist and Nobel Prize candidate, Rigoberta Menchu, or Brazil's Amazon defender, Chico Mendes (killed by a landowner in Acre Amazon state in 1988) and winner of the Global 500 Prize from the United Nations, or Sao Paulo's Mayor Luiza Erundina, or Maria Elena Moyano, leader of the popular canteens and the Glass of Milk committees integrated by 400,000 women. They represent not only important grassroots movements, but symbolise a twentieth century quest for human rights and social change in the face of great odds, and their presence and activism have enlarged the context of economic and human survival and development.

The economic double-bind

This new reality constitutes one of the most difficult and challenging socio-economic problems that the region's people have faced in recent times. Foreign debt and debt servicing, structural adjustment policies, economic recession and inflation have become a heavy mortgage on the future of Latin America, and the effects of all these factors have only been partially disentangled.

The origins of indebtedness can be traced to the early 1970s, when recycled petrodollars were loaned to the region at very low interest rates. Projects facilitated by the international financial groups (IFIs), were poorly conceived and inadequately evaluated. Investments were made in large unproductive infrastructures. Increasing military budgets, corruption (the region was basically administered by military regimes) plus the sudden stringent monetarist policies and the increase in real interest rates pushed by financial groups in the U.S., the U.K. and other industrialised countries, led the region to a crisis.

Just debt servicing increased from US$ 297 billion in 1981 to US$ 428 billion in 1990, according to the Inter-American Development Bank. This phenomenon was further aggravated by the low prices of export commodities produced by the region, losing its indicator of positive net transfer of resources of US$ 11.5 billion from the industrialised countries in 1980, becoming a net exporter of resources and capital to the industrialised countries since 1982.

Between 1982 and 1990 Latin America suffered a drain of US$ 223 billion; in addition, the region (including the Caribbean) devoted US$ 503 billion to the payment of the debt, of which US$ 313 billion went towards debt servicing, according to the U.N. Economic Commission for Latin America (ECLA).

In order to recover its external balance, the region was forced to reduce the import of investment goods and spare parts, thus making for a disinvestment in social infrastructure, roads and communication systems, and a general drop in net internal investment which was 26 per cent in 1990 when compared with the rate in 1981. All these indicators clarify why the decade of the 1980s has been called the 'lost decade', a loss which was utterly aggravated by the policies adopted in many countries, like Argentina and Chile, to liberalize domestic capital markets, thus allowing for a massive transfer of capital: about one-third of the total foreign debt of the region.

But if macro-economic indicators are overwhelming, their effects on the majority of the Latin American people, specially women and children, are even more dramatic; maternal mortality rates in some countries of the region are one hundred times higher than those of industrialized countries. Inflation indicators from the ECLA reveal that the consumer price index went from 1160 per cent in 1989, to 1490 per cent in 1990; add to this the level of unemployment and wage freezes, and we see that 185 million people in the region live on the brink of poverty. UNDP figures show that in 1990, 270 million people (62 per cent of the population) live in poverty. The scale of poverty varies from country to country and the UNDP draws a comparison between two Central American countries: poverty in Costa Rica hits 22 per cent of the families, while in Guatemala it affects 77.5 per cent.

The heavy social cost that Latin Americans have had to pay has favoured the creation of a parallel 'informal economy' which in fact saved the people from total collapse during the last 'lost' decade. It is precisely in this new economic context that women of the region have played a key role in what economists and technocrats have named 'invisible adjustment': a survival strategy sustained by the informal economy, basically managed and promoted by women through a multiplicity of economic solutions and expressions for survival. They range from the creation of co-operative movements and micro-enterprise, to popular canteens, self-cultivated orchards, the Glass of Milk committees, informal trade and a massive injection of dollars remitted by illegal immigrants to industrialised countries. The resilience and adjustability of women, in a concert of vitality and creativity, has staved off their families' and communities' starvation, surviving the body blow of drastic structural adjustments.

Nevertheless, the challenge is far from over, and the setbacks of the regional economy still weigh heavily on every new-born Latin American child who formerly was said to bring 'a loaf of bread under the arm' but now brings 'his own share of debt under the arm'.

Moreover, a political paradox has created a new dilemma for Latin Americans, even as they are torn between an internal strength for survival and the lack of response from their political leadership. While most regional political leaders have attained power through formal democracy during the last decade, the people seem to think that they can do without a formal democracy because, after all, it does not ever put into practice democratic social and economic solutions. For the impoverished population it is difficult to believe official and mainstream announcements of the arrival of democracy to the continent, merely on the strength of elections being announced. For their leaders do *not* democratically distribute the cost of the debt crisis and adjustment — a crisis which they may not have created but that they do perpetuate.

The final paradox is that sections of the impoverished population support the rise of initiatives like the recent presidential coup by the democratically elected Peruvian Premier, Alberto Fujimori, and the aborted military coup led by Lieutenant Colonel Hugo Chavez against Venezuelan President, Carlos Andres Perez; they forget that military regimes have been equally responsible for mismanagement and abuse in their own countries.

In the end, people seem to have adopted a mixture of scepticism and wisdom which might be expressed in the words of Albert Einstein: "Do not do anything that your consciousness does not dictate to you, not even if the State demands it."

Patricia Baeza

BOLIVIA

"Our coca is not cocaine"
Carmen Beatriz Ruiz

El Chapare — Enveloped in the dank air of Chapare, women gather the tiny, dark green leaves of the coca shrub with an expertise acquired over generations. These nondescript coca leaves are later processed to produce that most potent of narcotics, cocaine, on which drug cartels are built. Chapare, a sub-tropical region, wedged between the Amazonian plains and the slopes of the Andean mountain range, some 800 kms from the Bolivian capital, La Paz, supplies most of the country's coca. Estimates indicate that Bolivia is the world's second largest coca producer after neighbouring Peru. About 60,000 hectares are planted with coca bushes and nearly 370,000 families depend upon this crop for their livelihood.

It is also the most lucrative crop. The people of Chapare say that even the lowest price for a 'weight' (an inca weight varies from place to place) of çoca leaves is between four and ten times higher than the price of any other crop that could be grown in the region.

Lola Velez, executive secretary of the Bartolina Sisa (the national peasant women's federation), highlights the importance of the coca plant to farmers, particularly in the light of the prevailing economic conditions of Bolivia. Admitting that many women are involved in coca production, Velez explains,

"It's a family crop. These women know that their family's survival depends upon it." She, like the hundreds of peasant women she represents, is vehemently opposed to the militarisation of the anti-drugs war.

In April 1990, President Jaime Paz Zamora accepted 56 United States military advisers to train Bolivian troops in anti-drug tactics as part of a US$ 15 million aid package. This marked the Bolivian army's first entry into the drug war. The country's coca growers reacted sharply to this development. Head of the Chapare coca growers association, Evo Morales is on record saying, "When they approved the US presence here they declared war on us. If the military comes in, we will form armed groups to fight." Recently, Bolivian coca farmers warned the government that they would block roads in protest against the proposal to use the army in the drug war.

Nearly all peasant groups affiliated to Bolivia's Tupaj Katari peasant workers' confederation, have pledged themselves to this action. Interior ministry officials have announced that police and army units will patrol roads to prevent what the under secretary has described as "breach of peace". Velez feels that the army's entry is just an excuse to suppress the peasants. "And this violence of repression particularly affects women when the soldiers come and surround the houses or destroy the coca plantations. For this reason, women too will be actively involved in the blockade for the army," she says.

Local coca consumption has a thousand-year-old tradition among the Andean peoples, and it is both legal and considered harmless to health. According to official statistics, ten per cent of Bolivia's coca crop is consumed locally. The custom of chewing the leaves or preparing coca-leaf tea to ward off hunger and combat altitude sickness goes back to the days of the Inca civilisation. However, the cultivation of coca for export in El Chapare can be traced back to the early 1980s, when the centre of production shifted from the neighbouring province of Santa Cruz to this region in the province of Cochabamba. "Today, women not only work in large numbers as coca producers in the areas of Chapare and Los Yungas, but they also substitute the men who leave the arduous agricultural

work to improve their incomes by cultivating coca for export,"
explains Velez.

The peasants argue that they cannot be blamed for growing
a plant that they have been cultivating for generations simply
because others have transformed it into an addictive narcotic.
"Our coca isn't cocaine... They are the ones who make it so.
Our coca is medicine for the Yungas.." is the refrain of a
popular folk-song composed by a group of Yunga peasants.
Feeble attempts to encourage economic alternatives to 'excess'
coca production (a term used for coca illegally used by drug-
traffickers to manufacture cocaine) have made little headway.
And even official data reflects the fact that it is chronic social
neglect that has driven the local peasants to coca production.

In Chapare, for instance, there is one doctor for every
124,000 people, over half the population is illiterate and
children receive an average of 3.7 years of schooling. To date,
agriculture remains Bolivia's main economic activity but the
peasant is the lowest paid and agricultural workers are the
majority of workers.

And until conditions improve, coca, it appears, will continue
to feed hundreds of peasant families, and Bolivia's market
places will still teem with vendors selling coca leaves as their
cries of "Chewing leaves, chewing leaves" rent the air.

Squeezing tin out of rocks
Cecilia Crespo

La Paz — As the faint light of day creeps over the Andes
mountains, Eusebia Janco leaves her windswept 9,000 ft. high
camp to hack tin from the stones and rocks that lie heaped
outside the mining tunnels. Janco's husband died of silicosis,
a kind of tuberculosis that affects miners, several years ago and
she took to breaking rocks for a living. Janco is one of the
hundreds of miners' widows who are forced to take up menial
work in the country's tin mines to support themselves and their
families.

The work is back-breaking. "We have to work non-stop. It's

a very hard job and we're all old now," says 50-year-old Janco who lives in the "Siglo XX" (20th Century) mining district about 300 kms from the capital La Paz. Known here as palliris (a Quechua term meaning `gatherer'), these Andean peasant women perform an essential task in the mining industry scattered over the Bolivian Andes. They squat on the heaps of rubble and shards, breaking open rocks with hammers and home-made tools to extract fragments of tin from the stones. The palliris work for at least eight hours a day, regardless of rain and the biting cold, just to scrape together a few pounds of tin.

Bolivian mines have been around since Spanish colonial days. From the 1930s, tin became a leading export, accounting for 40 per cent of the country's total exports. The mines were later nationalised in 1952, when after several revolts and fraudulent elections, a national insurrection led by trade unions and peasants brought Jaime Paz Estenssoro to power. However, this system backfired and 30 years later the mines were declared bankrupt. A neo-liberal "relocation" policy was applied, which in effect meant that 30,000 miners lost their jobs. Recent talk of privatising the mines once again has led to hunger strikes by miners' wives in the desolate encampments of this South American country's mining areas.

Faced with an uncertain future, many mining families have moved down to the warmer valleys of Cochabamba and Las Yungas to work as coca pressers. Coca leaves are pressed underfoot in much the way grapes once used to be, to form the basic paste out of which cocaine is illegally processed. Ironically, it is this shadowy side of its economy which has helped Bolivia to recover slightly from the crushing economic effects of plummeting tin prices on world markets.

However, most palliris have set up their own cooperatives to continue with the only work they have ever known. Agriculture — even basic subsistence farming — is out of the question on these barren Andean slopes where temperatures often drop well below zero at nights. "We're palliris, but we're also mothers with warm blood and a beating heart," says Janco emotionally, "We're mortgaging our lives extracting tin because we love our children." Although they live in mud huts without water or electricity, the mining widows are proud to be Quechua, one of the two majority indigenous groups in Bolivia. The women share the little food they cook at home as well as the coca leaves, traditionally chewed to ward off hunger and cold.

Like most palliris, Janco, a mother of six, can barely read or write. But she can tell at a glance the different qualities of tin. At sundown she and her eldest son, David, aged 23, gather all the tin they have extracted during the day and hand it over to the cooperative. Sometimes they sell it to a private bank in Oruro town, about 200 kms east of La Paz. The 120 members of Janco's cooperative each get a monthly salary equivalent to US$ 50. Each palliris collects about two to three pounds of tin a day. "I work about 10-12 hours a day, but the money I get is little reward for the hard physical work," remarks Janco.

In 1970, the Central Workers' Union, Bolivia's main trade union, abolished this exhausting work that causes disease and death. But palliris have no choice but to continue to extract tin from discarded rocks. "Although output has been reduced because of falling prices, the amount of tin extracted has been maintained and in some cases, has even increased," says engineer Luis Prado, president of the national chamber of mining, adding that mining exports continue to be "one of Bolivia's main sources of foreign exchange".

But the enormous volume of tin produced (10,000 tons in 1991) is cold comfort to the thousands of men and women who sacrifice their best years — and often, even their lives — to the hostile mines of the Bolivian Andes.

BRAZIL

Bartering fertility for votes
Vera Lucia Salles

San Luis (Maranhao) — Increasingly, political candidates are bartering sterilisation for votes, promising women a glorious future, uncluttered by more children, in exchange for their precious votes. The practice is rampant, especially in Maranhao in northeastern Brazil, where the candidates, even while campaigning for elections, convince women to get themselves sterilised. According to Maria Gonzalves, a member of the San Luis Women's Group, "The sterilisations are usually carried out in government hospitals, regardless of medical consider-ations." Many women end up believing that this barter is the golden opportunity they have long been waiting for. As a 22-year-old woman with four children said: "I spoke to the candidate and it was very simple. He promised to arrange the operation if I voted for him. So he fixed me up with a visit to the Santa Lucia hospital and I was sterilised. After all, you can't keep filling your house with children, can you ?"

At least 7.5 million Brazilian women between the ages of 15 and 54 have been sterilised. According to figures from the Health Ministry and the United Nations Children's Fund Brazil's sterilisation rate has increased sharply, from 11.3 per cent at the end of the 1960's, to 45 per cent in 1990. The use of sterilisation as a contraceptive method is most widespread in northeastern Brazil, particularly in the state of Maranhao, where an alarming 79.8 per cent of the women are sterilised. Poverty, unemploy-ment, low salaries, lack of adequate health care and housing, together with ignorance of birth-control methods, lead many women to opt for sterilisation as a means of preventing the birth of children they simply cannot support.

Jenileia Rodrigues, 31, a street cleaner and voluntary health worker, is a typical case. "I had my tubes tied when I was 24, because I couldn't afford more children," explains Rodrigues. "I only knew about the rhythm method and a few home remedies. But these didn't work. I kept getting pregnant." The situation is even more difficult for very young women. Ana Cristina, a 19-year-old, was coerced into sterilisation by her mother, Guillermina Salles, a health worker. "I just couldn't stand it longer. From the age of 17, my daughter had one pregnancy after the other, even though she's unmarried. The house was full of kids, my husband, our six children and hers.

I was so relieved when she was sterilised," says the tired mother.

But perhaps the most insiduous use of sterilisation is as a tool of discrimination. According to Gonzalves, "Most women who have been sterilised are black. So, it is not just a question of social class, but of race." Lucia Regina de Azevedo, a member of the Black Cultural Centre and the Mae Andrezza Women's Group, feels that "sterilisation is being used to exterminate the black race". Together with other public and private institutions, the Mae Andrezza Women's Group has launched a campaign against the mass sterilisation of women, which will culminate in a meeting of black women in the northeastern state of Bahia, next month.

A similar campaign is also underway in Rio de Janeiro, sponsored by women's orgsanisations, cultural groups and black movements. These groups maintain that sterilisation has become institutionalised. The Rio forum believes mass sterilisation programmes are "sexist, classist, and racist" and call for government policies to improve life for working women. Eight years ago, the Permanent Forum Against Sterilisation, comprising 32 organisations, was established in Rio de Janeiro. The organisation has repeatedly denounced the involvement of international agencies in financing sterilisation projects in Brazil.

Between 1985 and 1989, the Pro-Life Association of Brasilia studied family planning programmes carried out in the country by international agencies. The study revealed that at least 20 organisations were funding voluntary sterilisation programmes and medical training in various parts of the country.

Graza Caetano, coordinator of the mother and child division of Maranhao's health department, acknowledges that sterilisation is commonly practised in public hospitals, and mainly on the poorest and least informed women. She proposes that "health centres should offer a counselling service for women on the various birth-control methods, so they can plan their families better." Although 27 provincial and community health workers received training between 1988 and 1990, general health care for women in San Luis has shown little improvement and few local clinics or medical centres provide effective family planning services.

The president of the Brazilian Society for Human Reproduction, Dr Hueidson, says that his organisation is pressuring the government for more campaigns directed towards marginalised women, so that they gain free access to various contraceptive methods. Hueidson, like many others, is quite confident that despite limited resources and large foreign debts, Brazil has the capacity not only to manufacture but also to distribute free contraceptives. If only this was pursued, Brazilian women could have more control over their reproductive system without having to barter it to the next political candidate that comes along.

CHILE

Sowing hope in family plots
Carmen Ortuzar

Santiago — For Lilian Rios, every tender green shoot of the celery, parsley, silver beet or carrots that she has planted is like one more child. The kitchen garden is her proudest possession as she nurtures her vegetables like she nurtured her own children. Rios is a fairly recent convert to kitchen garden projects which are gaining popularity in this South American nation.

'Family plots' as they are referred to, began to proliferate in the early 1980s, as women realised their potential in providing a simple, low-cost method of feeding large families. "One day a fieldworker visited me and explained how useful growing vegetables could be to someone like me with a large family and low wages. She said I'd enjoy growing my own vegetables", recalls Rios. The incorporation of Chilean women into new areas of agriculture is a recent phenomenon. In an effort to feed their families, women have accepted help from various official and religious institutions to set up their family plots.

Sarita Larrain was one of the first women to experiment with this system after training at the Colina Technical Centre, just north of the capital, Santiago. Larrain, in turn, trained Maria Montecinos and Irene Arredondo in how to build the large 6-by-20 metre boxes known as 'raised beds'. Like Rios, Larrain's two new recruits are overjoyed with their gardens. In these 'raised beds,' the women plant a large variety of vegetables including beans, silver beets, potatoes, onions, chillies, celery, carrots, lettuce, parsley, cabbage, and cauliflower. The beds provide enough vegetables for a large family.

According to a study entitled *Women's World, Continuity and Change* by Ximena Valdes of the Centre for Women's Studies, the increased participation of Chilean women has had a great impact on the country's agricultural sector. In 1980 more than 5 million hectares were dedicated to the cultivation of fruits for export. Fruit exports in the middle of 1980 were worth US$ 400 million. The success of agricultural exports has meant that many women are now employed seasonally, during harvest time. Fruit cultivation accounts for 84 per cent of Chile's agricultural output, and represents 12 per cent of total exports.

Although several agricultural organizations have their own statistics, the exact proportion of women employed as 'temporeras' (seasonal workers) is not known. However, seasonal agricultural workers are thought to number approximately 45,000, equivalent to the number employed in manufacturing. The expansion of the agricultural sector is a result of agrarian reforms introduced between 1963 and 1973. Further reforms later took place within a liberal economic framework.

Ideally the whole family should be involved in building the 'family plot,' for this type of intensive farming requires crop rotation throughout the year. The National Rural and Pastoral Commission, under the aegis of the Chilean Episcopal Church, has published a simple horticultural manual which the project uses for training. The manual suggests the sequence in which vegetables should be sown, harvested, and sown again to keep the soil productive. Since the plants extract large quantities of nutrients from the soil, it is essential to replace these continually, using natural compost to maintain the soil's fertility. The manual stresses the importance of taking care of the soil and urges people to make organic compost from left-over vegetables, ashes from fireplaces and bonfires, bio-degradable household rubbish and guano. This refuse is piled up in a corner of the garden or patio, or in a large aerated drum. The air and humidity soon turn the mixture into excellent organic fertilizer.

It is not known how many Chileans have their own 'family plots,' as this system has spread quickly, through relatives, neighbours and friends. The Commission's goal is to use family plots to "transform our problems of poverty, aggression and insufficiency into valuable riches, and help create a better world where hopes can flourish".

COLOMBIA

Indians march for salt
Angela Castellanos

Bogota — For the first time ever, Colombia's Indians may strike up a business partnership with the government. And if the deal works out, it will be largely due to the untiring efforts of a 35-year-old Wayuu Indian woman, Rosario Epiyeu. Epiyeu, who belongs to the minority Wayuu indigenous group, whose 100,000 people live along the Guajira peninsula in northern Colombia, is representing her community in negotiations with the state-owned salt mining company, 'Ifi-Concesion-Salinas.'

Salt production which has always been the economic mainstay of the Wayuu, was something they had developed to perfection long before the arrival of the Spanish conquistadors in the 16th century. For Wayuu Indians, salt is the very basis of their existence. According to local folklore, Mareiwa, the creator of humans, also made the land and the sea. When the sea covered the land, salt was formed and Mareiwa put the Wayuu here to harvest the salt. But this traditional belief received a shaking in September 1991 when the government of this South American country launched a salt production project and contracted the Colombian army to extend the dykes along the sea. Alarm spread through the Wayuu community because this project affected the 'ponds' or pools where the salt crystallizes, flooding the areas where the Wayuus work, extracting the salt.

The Indians were not going to take this lying down. They organised two protest marches to the town of Manaure, in which 4000 women (and not a single man) took part. "But then we heard about the proposed privatisation of the salt flats," recalls Epiyeu. "And this included our lands which are considered to be wasteland, despite the fact that we used this land long before they came along. So we decided to go to the capital to talk to the government."

The Indians' loss of control over the salt flats in the region has been very gradual. Even during the Spanish colonial period, some of the salt flats were appropriated by the Spanish crown. Much later, in 1968, the Colombian government took these over and established the Ifi-Consecion-Salisnas Company to exploit the salt deposits. The Wayuu were left high and dry, with just a few small ponds to harvest. "We've had problems with the company for years," complains Epiyeu. "About 20 years ago, they destroyed two marshes of nearly 4,000 hectares by turning them into artificial pools where sea water is collected for salt extraction. As a result of this we cannot fish anymore. They also damaged two freshwater streams and destroyed the forest."

Evidence of the ecological imbalance caused in the region is ample. Ten kilometres of a mangrove swamp were cleared, forcing the migration of many fish and bird species, including the stately flamingo. And over the last decade, the coast has visibly eroded. The local Indians — about 3,000 of them — who were hired by the state-owned company, were disgruntled. "They didn't even give us the necessary working tools and they paid us a pittance," Epiyeu recalls. But when the Wayuu

Indians began to exploit their own salt pools, the company called in the police. "They would suddenly arrive, snatch our bags and throw them into the sea," say the Indians. In 1988, when the company accused the Indians of competing against them, the Wayuu struck work and the company finally gave in to some of their demands of tools, drinking water and health services. "But now we have tuberculosis and the health centres don't have enough doctors or equipment to cope," Indian spokespersons point out.

The Ifi-Concesion-Salinas salt production covers not only the needs of 70 per cent of Colombia's domestic requirement and meets the demand of the country's chemical industry, but also leaves enough for export. Authorities admit that the Wayuu extract 200,000 tons of salt a year — half the amount registered by the state-owned company. So the Indians felt that they could work out some sort of a deal with the authorities. But there are several obstacles in the way. "We don't want to let go of our own traditions, and salt production is an integral part of it," explains Epinyeu. "Our argument is that the company owes us a debt for the marshes it took away from us which deprived us of income. So we're asking them to repay us by making us partners in the business." The Wayuu are also demanding property and ownership rights on the salt flats, compensation for "cultural damage" and a percentage of the profits from the salt exploitation.

"I've spent years working to help the community. I've even tried working with local politicians. But they only wanted votes. I would get them votes but they never helped us once the elections were over. Now Wayuu landowners have placed their trust in me to represent them," says Epinyeu. While they wait for the next round of negotiations, the Wayuu hope the government will realise that Indian groups and natural resources should not be sacrificed for economic development. But they also hope that salt can once more become the common resource it was before the Spanish came.

ECUADOR

Fewer children, less land
Consuelo Albornoz

Quito — The Tsachila Indians, one of the 16 remaining indigenous ethnic groups in this South American nation, are threatened with virtual extinction. Experts blame the low birth rate among Tsachila communities and the constant encroachment on their land by settlers and farmers, for this situation.

The Colorados — or Reds, as the Tsachilas are called because they paint their faces and bodies with a red dye extracted from seeds of the achiote plant —live in Santo Domingo de Los Colarados. This is a subtropical mountainous area, about 130 kms east of the capital, Quito. The region, near the country's Pacific Coast, has a total population of 210,000, with Tsachila Indians comprising only 1,800. According to recent figures, the Tsachilas currently live in eight communities concentrated in a 50 sq kms area, with only 5,000 hectares of land.

Zacarias Aguavil, a 32-year-old Tsachila farmer, echoes his people's dilemma when he remarks :"Colorados must not disappear. We must have more children to guarantee the survival of our culture. But on the other hand, we have very little land left. So we ask ourselves: If we have more children, where will they live?" Aguavil's neighbour, 25-year-old Gumersindo Aguavil, agrees.

"There is no more land for our children. Whatever little is left is tired and ruined from so much cultivation. I've been thinking of educating my children so that they can become doctors and find work. But then, they would have to live in the city," he says.

And this is the indigenous community's other predicament. The Shamans or elders as well as the young Tsachilas are in a quandary for they are all aware of the risks to their survival. While on the one hand sensing the need for educating their children, they also fear that if their youngsters are educated, they will be swallowed up by urban society, and thereby lose their cultural identity. According to official figures, literacy rates among the Tsachilas vary between 64 per cent in com-munities with schools and 11 per cent in communities without.

Anthropologist Guillermo Robalino, who spent several years living with the Tsachilas, says the Colorados' situation has got worse by the imposition of outside social patterns. "Faced with a serious land shortage, society encourages them to solve the problem by not having any more children. Contraceptives have been extensively promoted to cut down the size of the Tsachila Indians' families," he explains. However, Antonia Kakabadse, president of the Unity Foundation which works towards ensuring the survival of the Tsachilas, has a different point of view. "The Indians are a realistic people. When they say it is difficult to have more children because they cannot feed them, they are absolutely right. In fact, we have a project to repurchase some of their lands from settlers," he says.

In 1966, the Tsachilas owned 18,800 hectares of land. But by 1986, they had barely 8,800 hectares left with them. Almost 10,000 hectares had been taken over by settlers. "It is common practice for settlers to invade Tsachila areas to acquire cheap land. Some Tsachila communities have lost their land al-together," Robalino points out. To some extent, the country's agrarian reform laws have made this possible. The Tsachilas rent their land to settlers (a practice forbidden by their own laws) and after three years, the agrarian laws allow the settlers to retain possession of the land.

Moreover, until 12 years ago, birth control methods were being actively promoted among these communities by the United Andean Indian Mission — a private organisation which set up a family planning centre in Santo Domingo. Contracep-tion has drastically reduced the average size of the Tsachila families from 12 to 14 members to about 6 to 7. Nearly all the women use some form of contraception. Aguavil's wife, 24-year-old Rosa Maria, recalls her reasons for using birth control, "I did not want to get pregnant immediately after marriage, so I had an intrauterine device fitted at the family planning centre.

But that did not suit me at all, so I switched to the pill. After my second child was born, I just used the calendar method, but I got pregnant again. So I'm back to the IUD. It's not too bad this time. It only troubles me when I am doing heavy work."

Official figures reveal that in 1990, 48.47 per cent of the rural women and 51.52 per cent of the urban women in the Santo Domingo region used some form of contraception. Of these women, 26.74 per cent were between 20 and 24 years old, a mature age for Tsachila women who usually begin having babies when they are 15. 23.34 per cent of the women in this age group have two children, 22.87 per cent have one child and 11.62 have no children at all. There have been allegations, off and on, of forced sterilisations among some women in the area. "The general comment is that some Evangelical sects are still carrying on sterilisation on Tsachila women, but there is no proof of this," says Robalino.

There have also been many cases of cancer of the uterus, due to improper methods and inadequate follow-up. "After the sterilisations, some women from three communities developed cancer. I cannot say with certainty that the sterilisations were to blame, but it is remarkable to find such a high rate among the communities," Kakabadse remarks. Meanwhile, the Tsachila Indians of Ecuador continue to be among the endangered ethnic groups in the country, trying to find an effective way to counter a dwindling population and decreasing land simultaneously.

Shrimp industry destroys mangroves
Consuelo Albornoz

Esmeraldas — Shell-gatherers along Ecuador's Pacific coast are getting increasingly alarmed. Where once their baskets would overflow with shrimps, scallops, crabs and snails, they now find a mere handful of shellfish at the end of a tiring day. "Our

children won't be able to collect scallops and crabs anymore,"
sighs Jacinta Napo, as she displays her basket with the few
shellfish she has picked up after a long search among the
mangroves of Bunche province, where sea water and fresh
water mingle to produce a thick forest of mangrove trees.

Life, she says, used to be easy and there was always plenty
to eat. There was a time when they could find a hundred
scallops in five minutes. "Now you work from dawn to dusk
and you'd be lucky if you could get 200," says Napo, who has
gathered scallops for the last 10 years. The mangroves are
supposed to be state-owned "protected areas, but in practise
they are being "systematically destroyed by shellfish exporters," says Vicente Polit, president of the Tierra Viva (Living
Earth) environmental group. Ecuador's mangrove forests,
which grow along marshy coasts standing on roots that are
above the ground, have long sustained the eco-system here.
The trees have created a maze of waterways that serve as
perfect natural barriers against high tides and heavy swells, and
protect the coastline from floods. They have also been the
habitat of over 240 species of birds, reptiles, shellfish, molluscs
and fish, providing a rich source of food for hundreds of
families.

Today, Ecuador is the world's leading shrimp exporter. Last
year alone this tiny South American country exported about
75,000 tons of shrimp to the US, Italy, France and Spain,
earning over US$ 400 million. But the price Ecuador has had
to pay for this windfall is the slow devastation of its mangrove
forests. Even a law in 1985 banning further felling of mangroves failed to deter commercial shrimp producers, who
continue to build tanks for breeding shrimp. As a result,
mangrove forests are disappearing with frightening rapidity.
Within a year (1986-1987), half of the country's 362,832
hectares of lush mangroves was destroyed, as the local forestry
department, the district naval post and the fishing inspectorate
granted massive concessions to commercial shrimp-breeders.

"We have many decrees, many laws to protect the mangroves," points out lawyer Loudres Proano, founder of the
Committee for the Defence of Mangroves in the Muisne area,

"but they've all been broken with the full complicity of the authorities," as corruption percolates through every level here. In fact, as environmentalist Polit reveals, many of the shrimp-breeders are defence officers, with the right connections in the navy which controls marine resources. And those who issue the permits, says Polit, are totally unconcerned that "most of the concession areas are populated. There are communities that have been there from time immemorial, although they have no ownership documents or legal title to the land."

These are the people — especially the women — who are directly affected by the mangrove destruction. "Now we have only a tiny piece of the mangrove forest available to us," says 38-year-old Carmen Jacinta. "Sometimes the owners won't let us in to gather scallops. They threaten us with guns and dogs even though the navy has allowed us to collect shellfish." Collecting shellfish is exclusively women's work here. "It's hard work, that's why the men won't do it," Jacinta explains. "Besides, there's no other work here for women like me. I must earn my daily bread somehow to feed my five children."

Hard work apart, shell-gathering can be dangerous, with poisonous reptiles lurking in the dense undergrowth. Besides, many women develop rheumatism and skin diseases from standing for hours at a stretch in the muddy swamps. At the end of this they earn the equivalent of three US dollars a day, although their catch is highly prized in the cities. But they cannot compete with the powerful shrimp industry. "We're fighting a giant," remarks Proano, who feels the only way to halt the destruction is to set a legal precedent by at least denying concessions to the shrimp industry.

That, however, is like asking for the moon. Shrimp is this South American country's third major export after oil and bananas. According to official figures, shrimp production accounted for 4.7 per cent of Ecuador's gross national product last year. Profits vary according to production levels, but Polit estimates that a successful shrimp operation requires an enormous investment. "First you need to chop down the mangroves, move large amounts of earth, dig tanks and install a complex water pumping system. Then you need a range of products to regulate the salt-content and temperature of the water and its chemical composition, because shrimps are extremely delicate," he explains. Just a pump for the breeding tank costs about US$ 16,000, while labour and equipment costs to maintain a five-hectare tank costs an additional US$ 72,000. "But this expense can be easily recovered within a year and a half, as profit margins vary between 50-60 per cent," says Fredy Perez, president of Muisne's Committee for the Defence of the Mangroves. Latest figures show that Ecuador now has 1,500 shrimp-breeding tanks, 120 processing laboratories and 80 exporters occupying 175,000 hectares of mangrove. Yet, the industry employs only 10,000 permanent workers.

"We're not against the shrimp industry. We're aware it earns foreign exchange for the country," concedes Hernan Cortez de La Torre, another member of the Muisne Committee. "It is just that this industry has been established in the wrong place. The best place for it would be the salt-flats. But most of the shrimp companies are in the middle of the mangrove eco-system, causing immeasurable damage."

The Muisne Committee, together with other national environmental organisations, has launched a public information campaign to highlight the devastation of the country's mangroves. But members are well aware that changing public opinion is a long and tedious process. However, heartened by the fact that President Rodrigo Borja declared the 1990s as "the decade of eco-development," they intend to take their struggle to the highest authority in the land. They say they are not just defending the trees and birds which live in this eco-system, but "are against a destructive production system that pollutes the environment and impoverishes the people who use natural resources in a sustainable way".

EL SALVADOR

Conservation in the fields
Beatriz Maladonado

La Libertad — Environmental concerns have spread beyond El Salvador's universities and into the fields of La Libertad province about 20 kms from the capital, San Salvador. A group of women 'campesinas' (field workers) are organising their lives around a campaign to save this Central American nation's environment. A community run by ten women in Lourdes, in La Libertad, is busy building "compost latrines". They hope to counteract contamination of the water supply, recycle waste and address the problem of scant resources.

Seventy-five per cent of El Salvador's nearly seven million people have no sanitation facilities, 46 per cent have no access to safe drinking water and 49 per cent of all deaths are caused by parasites and infectious diseases, carried by polluted water supplies. The women were taught how to build compost latrines by members of the Palomera community, also in La Libertad province. The latrines consist of two cavities, one for urine and the other for faeces, which "reflect the anatomical nature of the human being", says Ricardo Navarro, President of the Salvadorean Centre for Appropriate Technology (CESTA).

CESTA is a non-government environmental organisation, one of 22 local groups which comprise the Salvadorean Ecological Union. The Centre is financed by the German Frederich Ebert Foundation. It also promotes ecological groups called 'grecos' among campesino communities, and sponsors conservation campaigns including the use of bicycles for transport in an effort to reduce air pollution. "The urine collected in the latrines is mixed with water and used as leaf fertiliser, while the excrement is mixed with ash or soil and buried for eight months, after which it becomes good organic compost," Navarro explains.

There are severe environmental problems in this small, densely populated country. El Salvador has an average of 230 people per sq. km. in a total area of only 21,000 square kms. According to conservation groups, 90 per cent of the country is affected by erosion, deforestation and air or water pollution. A 1986 survey reveals that Central America lost as much as 44 per cent of its tropical forests between 1950 and 1982. Estimated erosion rates in deforested areas in El Salvador are between 140 to 350 tons per hectare per year compared to 18 tons in the USA.

Alma Caraballo, coordinator of the Palomera environmental group, highlights the latrine project by pointing out that "it prevents contamination of water supplies due to the shallowness of the cavities, and provides cheap compost". The latrines cost US\$ 86.40 each, which includes the price of materials supplied by CESTA.

The children help their mothers build the latrines and also cultivate vegetables and soya beans to improve the community diet. Most Salvadorean campesinos eat beans and tortillas and have low protein intake. Guevara underlines the fact that the latrines lend to "a significant improvement in the communities which will be apparent in time". And Navarro adds, " The latrine project has encouraged the campesinos to organise themselves to solve their economic and housing problems, and has made them aware of the grave environmental dangers facing the country."

HONDURAS

Sowing seeds of hope
Thelma Mejia

Yolora — Under the hot sun, Lunila Varela carefully spreads manure on her new vegetable plot. This is her contribution to alleviating the chronic malnutrition that affects her small community, 100 kms south of the Honduran capital, Tegucigalpa.

Varela belongs to the "March 1st" group, which is affiliated to the Honduran Federation of Rural Women (FEHMUC), that is active in 16 of the 18 Honduran provinces. Despite internal organisational splits, FEHMUC is regarded as one of Honduras' most effective women's organisations.

FEHMUC, along with UNICEF, is working with local women on improving nutrition and sanitation, using alternative methods. An example is the vegetable-growing project, using discarded car tyres. First, a plot is demarcated then, a shade made from cane and clay erected to protect the plants from the sun. Old tyres are laid on the ground and used as fencing. The vegetable seeds and saplings are planted in the middle. "We never thought this would work. We said vegetables wouldn't grow here, because the sun is very strong and very hot. There's hardly any water, and besides, we've never grown our own vegetables before," says Varela, whose dried-out hair bears witness to the relentless Honduran heat - a major problem for farmers.

The south of the nation is one of the country's most disadvantaged regions, resembling a semi-desert area. Massive deforestation, indiscriminate wood-cutting in the few remaining forests, use of wood for salt production and large scale cotton cultivation, have dried out an already sun-baked land. The situation is so serious that environmentalists say the area should be declared an "emergency-zone", and warn that it could become one of Central America's first deserts. Until recently, because of the heat, the nine families from the hamlet of Yaloran subsisted on rice and beans. Any excess was sold or exchanged for other foods.

But now the land looks different.

The vegetable plots are full of nutritious radishes, tomatoes, sweet peppers, green beans, spinach, carrots and beets, which these families can add to their rather monotonous staples. "These newly introduced vegetables are substantially improving people's diets. Many of these communities used to eat just mango and plum leaves during the dry season," says Carlos Molinero, FEHMUC Project Coordinator and Supervisor for southern Honduras.

Nutrition is not the only problem that southern Hondurans are faced with. A UNICEF study reveals that 60 per cent of the people here have no access to drinking water, sanitation or health services. Agustina Garcia, from the community of Laure Abajo, in the southern province of Valle, weeps inconsolably. Her eight-month-old baby recently died from dehydration after bouts of acute diarrhoea and vomitting. "Women in the area have never had visits from the Ministry of Health's Medical Brigades, which are supposed to work in the area of preventable diseases. There is an urgent need for a community health centre to stop more children dying," says Beneranda Hernandez, a local FEHMUC activist. Despite the prevailing atmosphere of sadness in Laure Abajo, FEHMUC members speak enthusiastically of their numerous projects such as housing improvement, the vegetable plots, and small poultry projects.

Besides the benefits that FEHMUC has brought to the area, Hernandez feels, "the organisation has trained us, helped us organise ourselves, find ourselves and grow as women". Unlike other communities, the women in Hernandez's group in Agua Zarca have also involved their husbands in their projects. The men take care of the house and children when the women meet to organise and discuss the projects. Genaro Cruz, Hernandez's companion, says, " The women are very well organised, and we men realise this. We used to think once, that if women strayed from the house, they were encroaching on our territory . . ."

Greens protest against forest contract
Thelma Mejia

Tegucigalpa — Regina Osorio cuts a striking figure as she paces up and down outside the legislature in Tegucigalpa, with pine-cones in her hair and red carnations in her hands. This young, energetic television reporter belongs to a group of women environmentalists here who have launched their own distinctive form of protest regarding the fate of one of Honduras' largest forests. The women are incensed at an agreement signed in 1991 between the Honduran government and the Stone Container Corporation of USA. They believe this will allow the company to exploit a huge, one-million hectare tract of forest in Mosquitia, on the country's Atlantic coast.

Osorio, along with other green activists, spends her free time distributing "love-cones" to the public as a symbol of protest against a deal she regards as "damaging to national sovereignty". They station themselves outside the legislature in the Honduran capital, Tegucigalpa, urging passers-by to oppose the Mosquitia contract and handing out leaflets highlighting the plight of the country's forests. The deal with the US company "is an aberration which could rapidly wipe out our forests," says the journalist who has earned the respect of her colleagues for her excellent international television reports. "We must unite and fight to stop what appears inevitable — Congressional approval of the agreement — which will allow the exploitation for the next 40 years, of the country's main environmental 'lung'," urges Osorio passionately, as she presses a "love-cone" into the hands of a pensioner walking past the building.

Officially, the contract has been described as "sustainable management of forest resources". However, it is widely known that the contract was signed only two weeks after the US government cancelled a US$ 435 million debt owed on bilateral loans by Honduras. Although environmentalists and many others link the deal with the debt cancellation, the Honduran government emphatically denies the fact, declaring that national sovereignty is not negotiable "on any point".

But this does not convince anybody. Local as well as international green organisations fear that the US company will do away with Mosquitia's forests. And it will take at least another four decades to replace the trees felled for timber. Like all countries in this Central American isthmus, Honduras has suffered from relentless deforestation over the past two decades — a process that has decimated most of its pristine jungle areas. Today, only 3,997,000 hectares of forest remain, covering just 35 per cent of the country's 112,088 square kilometre surface. Although the government has refused to disclose the terms of its deal with Stone Container, environmental groups here believe that over a million hectares — nearly a quarter of the country's remaining forests — will be exploited.

Mosquitia is a lush area of rain forest, which, along with the Rio Platano Biosphere in northeastern Honduras, is the country's leading ecological reserve, harbouring many rare species. Pamela Wellnwer, of the US Tropical Forests Network, says the deal will jeopardise Honduras' flora and fauna and threaten rare species like the harpy eagle, panthers, pumas, jaguars and ocelots. She also points out how crucial the contract is for Stone Container, for it would help the company clear its current debt of four million dollars and even enable it to establish a subsidiary in Europe. But the government dismisses these claims as mere "propaganda aimed at discrediting (the US firm's) good record". It stresses that the company will exploit the forests responsibly to extract wood pulp and paper.

Wellnwer also cites US press reports saying that the Honduran government's economic advisor, Emin Abufelle and the ambassador to Spain, Rene Bendana, were involved in "behind-the-scenes" negotiations with Stone Container. It is alleged, says Wellnwer, that Abufelle will be "rewarded" by being put in charge of transporting all the timber, and Bendana by being appointed as Honduras' ambassador to the US. Her assertions have angered Abufelle, whom environmentalists have previously accused of scheming to import toxic waste into Honduras. "It's completely false that I'm involved in something as shameful as this," says Abufelle. "I'm also an environmentalist and I want the best for my country."

Wellnwer's courage in publicly denouncing government plans has given new strength to the local environmental movement which has doggedly, but so far unsuccessfully, opposed the deal. Little by little the country's feminist organisations have been adding their voice to the protest and have issued statements condemning the deal and supporting the green groups. So widespread has been public concern that even schoolchildren have sent letters to President Callejas, urging him not to "sell out" the country's sovereignty.

"Please don't sign the contract with Stone, because we want

to save our natural resources," wrote Dulce Maria Pavon, a schoolgirl from one of the capital's most marginalised districts. "Please excuse me, but you mustn't let them cut the trees. You should be proud to be the President of a country with such a beautiful reserve like Mosquitia. You want the money but we want the plants." Another child's letter says: "People think that because we're children we can't vote. But they're wrong because we're the future. Think carefully, Mr President. Just think what the world would be like without trees. It would be a nightmare and we don't want that. Please don't sign the contract."

But despite growing protests, all indications are that the government will in fact ratify the deal. The president of the Honduran legislature told WFS that the agreement would not be approved it if was considered harmful. However, if this was not the case, then "we believe it should be approved so we can start to make sustainable use of Honduran forests". The people of Mosquitia who learned of the contract a month after it was signed (the area's remoteness makes communication difficult), are now also opposing the plan. They are also becoming increasingly skeptical of the government's claims that the US firm will help the area to prosper.

Meanwhile, Osorio began receiving anonymous threats warning her not to continue with her protests. But she says: "I'm not intimidated. I'll keep on shouting until I'm hoarse." And the love-cones and red carnations will continue to win over more people to stop the contract and save the forests of Mosquitia.

MEXICO

Aids sweeps Jalisco
Yolanda Reyes

Guadalajara — Jalisco has always been famous for its ranchera songs which laud the machismo of its men. Sadly, it is also increasingly becoming known as the state with the largest number of AIDS-affected women in Mexico. While the national average shows one HIV-positive woman for every five men, in Jalisco the ratio is one for every 2.47 men. Jalisco, a few hundred kilometres northeast of the Mexican capital, tops Mexico's 32 states in the rate of HIV-positive women.

According to Dr David Diaz, coordinator of the health ministry's Council for the Care and Prevention of AIDS (CONASIDA), things have got so bad mostly because of indiscriminate purchase of blood by private blood banks during the 1980s. Desperate donors, including drug addicts and alcoholics, were willing to sell their blood for even a few pesos. Without disposable equipment in many of these centres, the AIDS virus spread rapidly. But it took years before Mexican health authorities closed down these centres. Then followed AIDS detection tests on all donors and blood received from other sources. But despite these efforts, health authorities have been unable to counteract the fatal effects of private blood banks. Life expectancy for Mexico's women AIDS victims is lower than for men, since 80 per cent of women like Martha, contracted AIDS — directly or indirectly — through transfusions.

Martha's case is fairly common in Jalisco. Her husband, a bricklayer, sold his blood on several occasions and contracted AIDS. He died two years ago, leaving Martha infected with a disease she had not even heard of until it was diagnosed. Today, this widow with five children has been totally rejected by her family who fear she might infect the others. Like all other mothers who find themselves in her predicament, Martha is especially worried about the fate of her children after she dies.

One of the factors contributing to increased AIDS among women, is the massive flow of Mexican migrants to the US. CONASIDA statistics show that in recent years, the number of women contracting AIDS through sexual intercourse has increased and now accounts for 30 per cent of the cases. Studies also reveal that women AIDS patients are less likely to survive than their male counterparts, due to psychological depression and additional social pressures they suffer on being told of their illness.

"We must remember that AIDS is usually labelled a sexual disease even though it is not always sexually transmitted," points out Dr Ajedandro Rodriguez. "Those infected are victimised and socially rejected, increasing their sense of isolation and lack of interest in life." Rodriguez, who has been treating AIDS patients for the last eight years, using medicinal herbs with very encouraging results, believes that the patients' state of mind has a major bearing on the development of the disease. Affection and psychological support, he feels, are essential to improve an AIDS victim's life and make the suffering less painful.

Teresa, a well-to-do divorcee with two children contracted AIDS from a US tourist who visited Jalisco briefly and died only months after leaving Mexico. A year after her relationship with the visitor, Teresa underwent a routine surgery which, surprisingly, led to serious complications. Her symptoms were diagnosed as AIDS and the knowledge simply shattered her.

In a telephone interview with WFS she expressed a complete lack of the will to live. But above all, she feared her children's reactions. "I've told them I had cancer. Sooner or later, I know they'll find out the truth, but I won't be around to see their reactions," she said.

About a year ago, Lourdes, a nurse working for the Mexican Social Security Institute (MSSI) in Jalisco, had a miscarriage and haemorrhaged with rapid weight loss. Doctors quickly diagnosed the symptoms as Aids. Analysis of her personal and clinical records revealed that Lourdes had contracted the virus while treating Aids patients at Jalisco's medical centre where she had worked on several occasions. Despite several petitions to the MSSI, Lourdes has not received any compensation since she is classified as an "informal worker" with the Institute. In an advanced stage of the disease, she too worries incessantly about her two small children.

Although CONASIDA has launched Aids prevention campaigns in Jalisco and some other Mexican cities, the rural population is still at great risk, largely because of the lack of information about Aids. Various non-governmental organisations involved in Aids prevention programmes have often described government campaigns in the media as "lukewarm and ineffectual". Moreover, ultra right groups such as Pro-Vida (Pro-Life), the conservative National Action political party as well as Catholic groups such as Opus Dei and Catholic Action, continue to protest against campaigns promoting the use of condoms, saying that they encourage promiscuity.

And despite the large number of cases, Mexico still does not have enough specialised hospitals to cater to Aids patients. In addition, Mexican women's ignorance about their own sexuality and Mexican men's traditionally irresponsible attitude towards contraception, spurs the further spread of the disease.

NICARAGUA

Biologists lead conservation campaign
Sylvia Torres

Managua — Three hundred and fifty Nicaraguan biologists and ecologists recently gathered on one of the country's main beach resorts to launch a campaign for environmental conservation. And just as well. It came as a surprise to most tourists at the beach that the plastic bags and tin cans which they habitually discard on the sand, would still be there next summer — and could even lie around for the next 200 to 450 years — before the forces of nature manage to rot and decompose them completely. Nicaraguan environmentalists, with financial backing from the legal representatives of large transnational companies such as Shell and Chevron, (who themselves are responsible for much damage to the environment), distributed waste containers and paper bags for a big rubbish clean-up. They also handed out leaflets urging people to keep the beaches clean.

Thirty-four year-old Patricia Caceres, biologist who organised these activities, is the director of the Biologists' Association of Nicaragua (ABEN). One of the group's main achievements was to succeed in forcing a ban, in 1987, on timber cutting and logging contracts in the basin of the San Juan river. It flows through the southern region of Nicaragua, and forms part of the country's border with Costa Rica. A large proportion of the clean-up brigades — about 80 per cent — was made up of women. Caceres believes that this was because tasks of cleaning and conservation are traditionally regarded as 'female' work.

Graduating as a biologist in 1979, she has been married for 12 years to an ecologist and feels very fulfilled working full-time at something which has been her passion since secondary school. "I was already clear about wanting to be a biologist when I enrolled at the university. I never asked whether it was a career in which you could make money," she declares. It was probably because of this ideology that when two years ago she was elected as Director of ABEN at a public meeting, she had no second thoughts about leaving her secure, well-paid job with the Ministry of Agriculture, Development and Agrarian Reform, to join a colleague as executive coordinator of ABEN's activities and programmes. "The environment has no parties or frontiers. The most dramatic example can be seen in the destruction of the earth's ozone layer. It doesn't just affect one particular country. It affects the planet as a whole," says Caceres. She adds that despite the regional conflicts in Central America, all environmentalists in the nations of the isthmus have remained united and in constant communication.

These close links with ecologists and biologists in neighbouring countries enabled the subsequent organisation of the Central American Congress for Environmental Action. Nicaragua's environmentalists have joined their Hounduran neighbours in protesting against the devastation of enormous tracts of forest, which have been cut down to make way for camps to accommodate the Nicaraguan counter-revolutionary troops and their dependents. Similar problems have arisen in Guatemala, El Salvador and Nicaragua, where military conflicts have caused damage to the environment and an imbalance in natural habitats.

URUGUAY

Weeding out the toxic harvest
Cristina Canoura

Montevideo — With valleys and plains, windmills and television antennas, Santa Lucia is a study in contrasts. And like its surroundings, the Santa Lucia Agricultural Cooperative (SALUCAL) faces the paradoxes brought on by modernisation. "Four years ago, we started getting together to see what we could do to reduce the use of pesticides and modern farming methods," says Carmen Marchissio of SALUCAL. The group has produced a report warning of the dangers of toxic agricultural chemicals. Pointing out the insidious manner in which pollution affects the lay person, Raquel Reyes, also of SALUCAL, says that in the area where she lives "people sell freshly sprayed vegetables, knowing full well that you're supposed to let one month go by before selling them".

SALUCAL was established in 1966 "to see if strength in unity really works" and to sell the produce of small farmers in the wine-producing area of Canelones province, about 60 kms from the capital, Montevideo. In sheer economic terms, the results have been positive. SALUCAL is now an industrialised cooperative, and in 1991 alone, processed 630,000 kgs of fruit. But although it is the cooperative's wine, bearing the name "The 27" which is now sold extensively in southeastern Uruguay, the group has dwindled over the years. Of the large numbers initially involved in the collective venture, as the name suggests, only 27 remain.

"We do a bit of everything, even kill ants that destroy the crop. We don't work alongside our husbands, but when we're done with household chores, we help out with everything, except spraying the pesticides, which the men spray with machines and on tractors," says one of the women. Most of the women interviewed are not members of the cooperative. But they are all closely involved in caring for the vines and harvesting the grapes.

This region grows a wide variety of vegetables, including potatoes, sweet potatoes, leafy vegetables, onion, garlic and tomatoes. It also produces most of the country's black tobacco. And as many of the women readily admit, herbicides are being increasingly used for all these. But for those whose livelihood depends solely on selling these vegetables, the negative aspect of pesticides and fertilisers takes a back-seat. "What can you do if the vines are diseased and you don't treat them? You lose them and you lose all the money invested. The same is true of fruit and vegetables," explains Reyes.

In 1990, SALUCAL organised a lecture on pesticides and invited experts from the faculty of medicine and chemistry. "It was wonderful" recalls one of the women. "Posters were distributed all over the province and we invited everyone. But more professionals from the city turned up than the people who actually use pesticides." Although the women have not been too successful in reducing the use of pesticides, they are well aware of the future risks to people, particularly children. At least this much has been achieved. "It's sad, but many people don't know what they're using. Perhaps they think there's no alternative, or don't realise that they're at risk," remarks one of the group's activists.

Dr Mabel Burgher, director of the toxicology department at Montevideo University, paints a far more alarming picture. Burgher's department carried out a research project with a group of city dwellers who were not involved with farming and had never handled pesticides. Clinical tests revealed residual organophosphate in their blood. Blood tests of several newborn babies and nursing mothers showed the same results. Burgher says her department deals with nearly 4,000 acute intoxication cases each year, caused by accidental ingestion of chemicals at work or at home.

Analysis of cases referred to the department reveal that pesticide poisoning reaches its highest levels between November and June (the period for spraying the crops). And the most severe cases, many of them fatal, are caused by phosphates.

"These occur mostly among agricultural workers who do not take the necessary precautions. Despite instructions and warnings on the containers, many youngsters spend the whole day spraying pesticides wearing only shorts. They use no protective clothing or masks," Burgher points out. Her research concludes that the population of this South American nation, like that of many other countries, "is impregnated with organochlorates, ingested mainly through food, but also through water and air."

However, on the brighter side, some positive examples of non-polluting agricultural techniques are slowly beginning to emerge. In the northeast of Canelones province, 50 women who have formed a group they call 'For Tomorrow' are growing organic vegetables for themselves and their families, and herbs for commercial sale. Instead of spraying the aromatic herbs with pesticides, the women use infusions of tobacco, crushed rue and nettles. They are now also building a solar drier to process the herbs naturally.

For Tomorrow has truly taken over the task of environmental educators and their advice is often sought out by local agricultural schools as well as producers of radio programmes for farmers. Although this 'green' trend has not yet gained a major following, Montevideo already has an agroecology movement, comprising non-governmental organisations and urban women's groups. Hopefully, the information they disseminate about alternatives, such as natural farming methods and traditional practices which have fallen into disuse, will spur more farmers into moving away from pesticides.

Building homes and communities
Christina Canoura

Montevideo — Displaying a high degree of skill, women have built many of Uruguay's Cooperative Housing Projects. Over 10,000 families in the country have had their homes built with the help of women labourers, who have done everything from laying parquet floors to tiling bathrooms and kitchens.

This South American country with a population of 3 million, has an estimated shortage of 120,000 homes and 40 per cent of all houses have no electricity, running water, or sanitation. During the 1970s, workers began to organise themselves to resolve their housing problems. The first Cooperative Projects were spearheaded by the Lanasur textile workers. One hundred and seventytwo families built the 'Covmit 9' Housing Project (Matriz Textile Housing Cooperative) in the Capital, having waited eight years before the bank approved their mortgage. This is not an isolated effort, however, eightythree similar housing projects exist in Montevideo alone, and another 35 are scattered in other parts of the country. 25 more are being legally processed, six are under construction, and 120 projects are being planned.

Although the architectural work was carried out by the Cooperative Centre of Uruguay (CCU), which offers legal and technical advice to its members, the families were also consulted on certain aspects of the design. The women from the Covmit 9 Housing Project were involved in every stage of the construction, except for digging the water wells and laying the roof tiles. "Supports were made for the joists, which were then lifted into position and filled in. The women were climbing up all over the place," recalls Eda, a member of the Covmit 9 Project. "We even cut through steel girders, once we'd learned how to use the cutting machine," she adds. The men mixed the cement and filled the moulds to make the blocks. The women would take the dried cement blocks out of the moulds when they were ready.

Each family pledged 21 hours of labour per week. Women had a weekly quota of five hours, but many of them also worked some of their husbands' hours. Many single women, like textile workers Milka and Ester, also worked on the scheme. They each put in 105 hours per month at bricklaying and tiling. "It was something we had to do. We pushed ourselves to the limit and struggled on, thinking this was our only chance to have a home of our own," says Ester, who is now retired. Some women took turns working as guards. During the day they would patrol the building site in groups of two or three for six hour shifts, distributing water and handing out the tools. All the tiling in the bathrooms and kitchens was done by women, as their labour was far cheaper than that of hired workers. "The foreman used to say we were much better at this type of work, that the tiles were meticulously laid," says Delia, another Covmit 9 member.

The money that was saved on the labour was spent on a special kind of tile cement. A team from the company that manufactures the cement trained four or five women, who in turn trained others. Eight years after the complex was finished, the women proudly claim that not a single tile has come unstuck. The women also helped build a nursery, a community room, a canteen, a library, and some commercial premises which have been rented out to small businesses. The nursery caters to 34 children from the complex and the local neighbourhood, and takes babies from the age of six weeks.

After the early days of euphoria, the Covmit 9 women admit they have recently noticed a certain apathy in the cooperative. "At first everyone struggles for a common goal. Once that is achieved, people seem to move apart and go their own way," says Lilian, a cooperative member. Despite the problems, the women recognise the benefits of the community effort. "Although we live our own lives, we don't have the feeling of loneliness we had before in other neighbourhoods. Here, if your child is ill, you can knock on someone's door at all hours, and know that they'll come to help you out,' says Alicia.

The families have also begun buying food in bulk to cut costs. "After finishing the house, many of us felt the need to carry on with something else. We had problems. But we've survived them and the group continues. And at the end of every year we have a big gathering to eat together," says Delia.

Index